Liam O'Flaherty

THE IRISH WRITERS SERIES
James F. Carens, General Editor

TITLE	*AUTHOR*
SEAN O'CASEY	Bernard Benstock
J. C. MANGAN	James Kilroy
W. R. RODGERS	Darcy O'Brien
STANDISH O'GRADY	Phillip L. Marcus
PAUL VINCENT CARROLL	Paul A. Doyle
SEUMAS O'KELLY	George Brandon Saul
SHERIDAN LEFANU	Michael Begnal
AUSTIN CLARKE	John Jordan
BRIAN FRIEL	D. E. S. Maxwell
DANIEL CORKERY	George Brandon Saul
EIMAR O'DUFFY	Robert Hogan
MERVYN WALL	Robert Hogan
FRANK O'CONNOR	James Matthews
GEORGE MOORE	Janet Egleson Dunleavy
JAMES JOYCE	Fritz Senn
JOHN BUTLER YEATS	Douglas Archibald
LORD EDWARD DUNSANY	Zack Bowen
MARIA EDGEWORTH	James Newcomer
MARY LAVIN	Zack Bowen
OSCAR WILDE	Edward Partridge
SOMERVILLE AND ROSS	John Cronin
SUSAN L. MITCHELL	Richard M. Kain
J. M. SYNGE	Robin Skelton
KATHARINE TYNAN	Marilyn Gaddis Rose
LIAM O'FLAHERTY	James O'Brien
IRIS MURDOCH	Donna Gerstenberger
JAMES STEPHENS	Brigit Bramsback
BENEDICT KIELY	Daniel Casey
EDWARD MARTYN	Robert Christopher
DOUGLAS HYDE	Gareth Dunleavy
EDNA O'BRIEN	Grace Eckley
CHARLES LEVER	M. S. Elliott
BRIAN MOORE	Jeanne Flood
SAMUEL BECKETT	Clive Hart
ELIZABETH BOWEN	Edwin J. Kenney
JOHN MONTAGUE	Frank Kersnowski
ROBERT MATURIN	Robert E. Lougy
GEORGE FITZMAURICE	Arthur E. McGuinness
MICHAEL MCCLAVERTY	Leo F. McNamara
FRANCIS STUART	J. H. Natterstad
PATRICK KAVANAGH	Darcy O'Brien
BRINSLEY MACNAMARA	Raymond J. Porter
AND GEORGE SHIELS	
STEPHEN MACKENNA	Roger Rosenblatt
JACK B. YEATS	Robin Skelton
WILLIAM ALLINGHAM	Alan Warner
SAMUEL LOVER	Mabel Worthington
FLANN O'BRIEN	Bernard Benstock
DENIS JOHNSTON	James F. Carens
WILLIAM LARMINIE	Richard J. Finneran

LIAM O'FLAHERTY

James H. O'Brien

Lewisburg
BUCKNELL UNIVERSITY PRESS

Associated University Presses, Inc.
Cranbury, New Jersey 08512

Library of Congress Cataloging in Publication Data

O'Brien, James Howard, 1919–
  Liam O'Flaherty.

  (The Irish writers series)
  Bibliography: p.
  1. O'Flaherty, Liam, 1897–
PR 6029.F5Z8   823'.9'12   78–126291
ISBN 0–8387–7772–4
ISBN 0–8387–7773–2 (pbk)

Printed in the United States of America

Contents

Preface 7

Acknowledgments 9

Chronology 11

1. An Aranman's Odyssey 15

2. O'Flaherty as Novelist 35

3. The War Novels 58

4. The Irish Psyche after the Revolution 72

5. The Short Stories 92

Selected Bibliography 118

Preface

For far too long the name of Liam O'Flaherty has
been associated primarily with *The Informer* (1925)
and the 1935 film based on the novel. Recently and
fortunately, however, O'Flaherty has been gaining a
new reputation among Irish writers—for his short
stories. These brief, lyric sketches, the bulk of which
were written in the 1920s and early 1930s, dramatize,
with directness and immediacy, elemental instincts of
man. O'Flaherty writes of peasants, children, and animals, without analysis or decoration, restricting himself
to the event, the object, the person, or the spoken word.
By paring away layers of civilization, and by avoiding
the intricacies of ratiocination, he reveals an elemental
harshness, brutality, pathos, or beauty. The passions of
men, the storms of nature, and the appetites of animals
run their inevitable course, often resulting in violent
death, before the equilibrium of nature is restored.

In addition to these short stories that we are coming
to see as his greatest achievement, O'Flaherty is the
author of fourteen novels, some of which are taut, almost ruthless probings of the traumas that produce an

Liam O'Flaherty

assassin, a puritan, a martyr, or a rebel—those torn spirits of the modern age that harass Ireland and the western world. Like other Irish writers, O'Flaherty has demanded our attention in autobiography, especially in *Shame the Devil,* a study of a writer's struggle to regain his creative powers. In whatever he has written—story, novels, and autobiography—O'Flaherty provides perceptive descriptions of the peasant in transition from an almost medieval world to the complexities of the twentieth century. Certainly no other writer describes in as great detail the varieties of social change affecting the Irish countrymen at the turn of the century.

Acknowledgments

Grateful acknowledgment is made to the A. D. Peters and Company, Literary Agents, London, for permission to quote material from the following books by Liam O'Flaherty: *Two Years, The Puritan, Shame the Devil,* and *Famine;* to Harcourt Brace Jovanovich Inc., New York, for permission to quote from *The Assassin.* I also thank the Bureau of Faculty Research, Western Washington State College, for a summer grant to complete work on this study.

Chronology

1896   Born August 28 at Gort na gCapall, Inishmore, the eighth of nine children.

1908–   Attended Rockwell College, Cashel, County
13   Tipperary.

1914   Attended Dublin Diocesan Seminary (Holy Cross College), September to November.

1914–   Attended University College, Dublin.
15

1915–   A member of the Irish Guards, enlisted under
17   the name of William Ganly, his mother's name. Wounded in September, 1917.

1918   Invalided out of military service. Received B.A. (War) from University College, Dublin.

1918–   Traveled and worked in South America, Tur-
21   key, Canada, United States.

1923   *Thy Neighbour's Wife* published.

1924   *Spring Sowing, The Black Soul* published. One of the founders of *To-morrow* (two issues, August and September).

1925   *The Informer* published.

1926   *The Tent, Mr. Gilhooley* published. Married to Margaret Barrington.

1927   *The Life of Tim Healy* published. Birth of daughter, Pegeen.

1928   *The Assassin* published.

1929   *The House of Gold, The Mountain Tavern and Other Stories, The Return of the Brute* published.

1930   *Two Years* published.

1931   *The Puritan, I Went to Russia* published.

1932   *Skerrett, The Wild Swan and other Stories* published. Founder Member of the Irish Academy of Letters.

1933   *The Martyr* published.

1934   *Shame the Devil* published.

1935   *Hollywood Cemetery* published. Received Academy Award for *The Informer*.

1937   *Famine, The Short Stories of Liam O'Flaherty* published.

1946–   Moved about between Ireland, England, and
52   France.

1946   *Land* published.

1948   *Two Lovely Beasts and other Stories* published.

1950   *Insurrection* published.

1952–   Settled permanently in Dublin. Made several trips to the Continent.

1956   *The Stories of Liam O'Flaherty* published.

Liam O'Flaherty

1

An Aranman's Odyssey

Unlike Yeats, O'Casey, and other Irish writers who turned to autobiography in their later years, Liam O'Flaherty wrote two volumes of autobiography as a relatively young man. Written partly because of financial need, *Two Years* (1930) and *Shame the Devil* (1934) nevertheless serve as revealing portraits of O'Flaherty. In the first volume, we see him as a war casualty and world tramp, and, in the second volume, as a successful writer striving to recover his creative powers. Although these books contain valuable insight into O'Flaherty's background and thought, they blur or ignore many events, especially conflicts that must have been of first importance to him as an artist. In the two books O'Flaherty creates a *persona* of an impetuous, extravagant young man, brimming over with physical strength, a man who has lost faith in his religion and civilization and is compelled by inner necessity to reformulate a faith as he writes his novels and stories.

Unfortunately, more particular and detailed biographical data on O'Flaherty is still limited. But in his

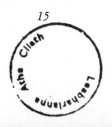

development as a writer two facts are preeminent: his birth into a peasant family on Inishmore, the largest of the Aran Islands, and his discovery of his native area as his literary material. O'Flaherty was born on August 28, 1896, in Gort na gCapall, literally "the field of the horses," in the northwestern part of the island, almost beneath Dun Aengus. Several details of the O'Flaherty family life appear in his brother Tom's book, *Aranmen All* (1934). The family was large, and several of the children died in infancy and early childhood. The father was a Fenian and a Land Leaguer who apparently forgot at times his obligations to his large family. An incurable rebel, the older O'Flaherty harassed the landgrabbers on Aran and was the first Sinn Feiner on the island. According to Tom, villagers gathered every evening in the O'Flaherty house for stories, song, and discussion, and his father was the best dancer on the island, and his mother, the best singer. Analogues to some of Liam's stories may be found in Tom's reminiscences and also in Tom's second book, *Cliffmen of the West* (1935), stories about the Aran Islanders at the turn of the century. Liam O'Flaherty speaks of his mother's gaiety and of her story-telling, at times a means to divert the hunger of her children. He also recalls her lifelong combat against poverty, relieved partially by the memory that her husband stole her away from a mainlander just as the latter arrived to sue for her hand. The O'Flaherty children attended school at Oatquarter under the schoolmaster David O'Ceallaghan, the prototype of the teacher in *Skerrett,* one of O'Flaherty's best novels. While Liam was still at school on Aran, a visiting priest of the Holy Ghost Order, Father Naugh-

ton, persuaded him to prepare for the priesthood.

From 1908 to 1913 O'Flaherty attended Rockwell College, County Tipperary, a college in which the Holy Ghost fathers trained missionaries for Africa. Here he earned several prizes, which, with his scholarship, helped to pay his fees. From September to November, 1914, he was at the Dublin diocesan seminary, Holy Cross College, and in 1914 to 1915 he was enrolled at University College, Dublin, receiving a bachelor of arts degree from that institution in 1918 under provision for men serving in the war. O'Flaherty's formal education bred in him a hostility toward the classroom, yet when asked for his special subject in regard to a teaching position in Rio de Janeiro, he replied, "The Classics." There is a report that he taught Greek in Brazil. But like Hemingway, O'Flaherty disdains learning as a layer of civilization that inhibits the development of the instincts. In addition, O'Flaherty became a bitter anticleric, especially in his nonfiction. He speaks of leaving a seminary in a rage because he would not wear the soutane; and he recounts ironically that the rector chided him, saying that O'Flaherty received a free education under the pretense of preparing to be a missionary.

In 1915 O'Flaherty joined the Irish Guards and served until he was wounded and shell-shocked at Langemark in September, 1917. He later said that his enlisting in the British army irritated the people of Aran much more than did his leaving the seminary. Certainly his military service is the watershed of his early manhood. His induction and training at Caterham Barracks opened a new kind of hell for him. The coarse language, his fight with an Argentine cowboy who knocked him out, and intensive drill to the motto "You'll go out of this gate a corpse or a guardsman" radically changed his understanding of himself and others. Under a sometimes brutal facade, he found a vigorous humanity. As a soldier he discovered his highly trained intellect a detriment: "I who had until then worshipped the mind to the extent of neglecting the body, now worshipped the body to the neglect of the mind." Under duress, he came to admire discipline and was proud of his regiment.

In France, O'Flaherty was assigned a dead man's place; he was "a new patch on an old garment," he said. But he writes of trench warfare in only one of his novels, *The Return of the Brute* (1929), and hardly at all in his short stories. In *Shame the Devil,* he describes the effect of his war injuries, his struggle to speak and inability to produce intelligible sound, and his being treated as a child or idiot. He was locked in a cell with iron bars on the window. Although he was then far removed from the battlefield, he worried about a transport officer whom he was to guide to the front line, his duty just before he was wounded. He later learned that he had been unable to speak from the time of his injury until an attendant poured water on his head as he rushed to strike a doctor. Finally he was discharged from King George V Hospital, Dublin, his disability called *melancholia acuta.* O'Flaherty flagrantly ignored the advice of doctors to avoid hot climates and any blows that might come to his head. At age twenty-one, scarred in body and mind, he became a bewildered civilian, cast back into a world in which he had no place.

In *Two Years* O'Flaherty looks back on his wander
years, actually the three years from August, 1918, to
1921. During this period he worked at almost every
kind of unskilled job on three continents. Many of
these jobs, it is true, lasted only a day or two, at times
just long enough for O'Flaherty to insult a foreman or
manageress. Besides serving as a fireman and a deckhand
on freighters, he was an assistant foreman in a brewery,
a hotel porter both in London and New York, a farm-
hand for a French-Canadian family, a lumberjack, a
carpenter, a Western Union messenger, a pastry maker,
a ditch digger, and a hand in a condensed-milk factory
and in a tire factory. Proud of his restored sanity and
physical strength, he endured the mockery of sailors
when he wore white pants for his first day of work as a
coal stoker. At times O'Flaherty reveled in the rough
life of a stoker: ". . . I began to enjoy being a trimmer.
I grew hard. I no longer minded the stifling heat, or the
terrific work. I felt equal to my comrades, and could use
oaths as foul as theirs. My habits became just as coarse.
I wolfed my food like a god, developed contempt for
dirt, and ceased to think or to be sensitive about myself"
(*Two Years*, pp. 89, 90).

O'Flaherty's appetite for fresh experience was enormous; he developed, along with his sharp tongue, a
remarkable capacity for retreating from difficulties.
Under the hiring arrangement of a Canadian nickel
mine, he was to be grouped with other workers according to his religion. O'Flaherty called himself a Zoro-
astrian and insisted on the validity of his choice, but the
perplexed manager placed him "with a nice set of
Methodists." As a former seaman, O'Flaherty falsely

claimed a knowledge of knots and accordingly was given charge of a scaffolding gang that was working on a smelter. O'Flaherty muddled his way through the raising of the scaffolding, but he had no idea of how to get the men down. Instead of calling for help, he fled the job, leaving the men in midair.

During the years of 1918 to 1921, O'Flaherty said that he lived mostly on the physical plane, working hard and drinking hard. His account of debauches on the beaches of Rio de Janeiro and of drinking contests in Smyrna, where he had delirium tremens, attest to his desire to outdrink hardened sailors. At this time O'Flaherty said that he was intellectually paralyzed. But on a drunken spree in London he was robbed of all his money, fifteen pounds. This loss jolted him out of a faith in a provident God. Until that time he "had been terrified and shocked because God did not exercise his omnipotence to punish evil and reward virtue." He concluded that there was no good and evil; experience was good and innocence evil. He gradually built a view of God and nature that informs much of his fiction:

> I am convinced that the divinity in man's destiny is his struggle towards the perfection of his species to a state of godliness. And that the most perfect types of manhood are always in revolt against the limitations of man's nature, his position on the face of the earth, and his ignorance. Towards the end of remedying these defects in man's structure and powers, *good* men have always struggled, and always shall struggle, to cleanse the blurred compass of man's intellect, that it may make manifest all the degrees of knowledge in the universe. They also strive to keep the race on the march towards perfection in all ways, by moulding new social institutions, new philosophies, new concepts of beauty [*Two Years*, p. 198].

In his fiction, O'Flaherty has many heroes "in revolt against the limitations of man's nature, his position on the face of the earth, and his ignorance." Generally these are large, tormented men blinded to that part of themselves or society lying outside their special dream of perfection. Each religion, O'Flaherty says, expresses its dream of perfection in its concept and images of the Godhead; to him man is evolving, climbing toward a perfection that is most fully expressed in works of art.

At the end of the wander years, O'Flaherty was depressed and broken in spirit; he required a spiritual renewal that could not be earned through physical work and riotous drinking. Bereft in Dublin, he followed a doctor's advice to return to the Aran Islands. At first, O'Flaherty said, ". . . I was like a ghoul, speechless, gloomy, a companion of the rough winds and breakers." He finished his long journey for recovery in his birthplace, seeking what the wide world could not provide: "A godless hermit, I began my communion with the cliffs, the birds, the wild animals, and the sea of my native land." O'Flaherty transformed this experience of finding a ground of being in nature and among simple people in one of his best novels, *The Black Soul* (1924) .

Yet O'Flaherty discovered a second faith to which he was partially dedicated for several years, that of Communism. He was not merely a literary Communist. In Canada O'Flaherty was inspired by the simple, intense dignity of men who spoke for the International Workers of the World, known as the Wobblies. With his friend John Joseph Peterson, who introduced him to the organization, O'Flaherty was fired from a lumber camp for trying to indoctrinate the workers. Several years before, as a university student, O'Flaherty neglected lectures to spend two weeks at the National Library reading the works of Karl Marx. With the help of his brother, O'Flaherty became associated with the James Connolly Club in Boston, where he read further in proletarian literature. For a short time he became a militant Communist: "In the early part of 1922 I seized the Rotunda in Dublin with a small army of un-employed men. We hoisted the red flag over the build-ing and held it for some days. Then we were driven out, and I fled to Cork with two companions" (*Shame the Devil,* p. 22). In *The Wild Geese,* Gerald Griffin recalls that on January 18, 1922, he saw the red flag flying and an enormous crowd converging on the build-ing. He was told that Liam O'Flaherty was commander-in-chief but that his official title was "Chairman of the Council of the Unemployed." O'Flaherty and his men held the building for three days, and each day the crowds became larger and larger, although there was no violence. Finally, at nightfall on January 21, O'Flaherty was told that if he did not take the men out of the Rotunda the police would force them out. To avoid bloodshed O'Flaherty gave orders to evacuate the build-ing.

O'Flaherty was attached to the Republicans briefly during the Civil War of 1922–23. He recalls a scene in O'Connell Street, Dublin, when the Free State troops captured the Republican headquarters in June, 1922, the day after he had been disbanded. Standing in a crowd, O'Flaherty overheard an old woman say that the bloody murderer Liam O'Flaherty had been killed, that he had locked the unemployed in the Rotunda and shot those who would not spit on the crucifix. Ironic enough to appreciate the absurdity of her tale, he was also realistic enough to be unimpressed by promises of Republicans that flying columns would sweep the country. He departed soon afterward for Liverpool.

Because of his dedication to Communism and his experience as a laborer, O'Flaherty might be expected to write about the exploitation of the working classes. But while his sympathies lie with the common people, he rarely writes of the laborer and apparently did not sustain his interest in the poor of Dublin. He found his material as a writer apart from the Communistic movements of the 1920s. His first work, he said, was a group of stories written after he had read de Maupassant in Connecticut, but these stories were rejected, and he did not write seriously again until he returned to London after his recovery on the Aran Islands. His vocation as an Irish writer was confirmed, he said, by an experience in London. As he was walking on the streets, he thought how beautiful it would be to stand on a cliff in Aran "watching the great waves come thundering to the shore, while the pure wind swelled my lungs." He rushed to his lodgings, knowing that he must be the spokesman for his people: "It seemed as if the dam had burst somewhere in my soul, for the words poured forth in a torrent. They came joyously and I felt exalted by their utterance, just as I used to feel when telling my mother some fantastic tale in my infancy." This revelation resulted in *Thy Neighbour's Wife* (1923), a novel that includes his most detailed description of peasant life on the Aran Islands. A promising rather than a fully successful work, this novel brought

O'Flaherty the help of Edward Garnett, the novelist, publisher's reader, and friend of Conrad, D. H. Lawrence, and others.

H. E. Bates, the novelist and short story writer, furnishes a description of O'Flaherty as a young writer in London. Bates recalls the vigorous presence of O'Flaherty at a dinner with Edward Garnett, saying that O'Flaherty was "a virile and impassioned Irishman who, rather like me, had a facile demon in him":

> O'Flaherty, true Irish, could talk a donkey's hind leg off and with fierce, blue, unstable eyes would stand in the middle of the room and begin reciting flowing nonsense from some as yet unwritten book, about 'women pressin' their thighs into the warm flanks of the horses,' until he codded you that it had really happened and was really true. O'Flaherty had arrived in London with a firebrand swagger, a fine talent and a headful of rebellious fury about the English and had sat down to write pieces of episodic violence about London, which he hardly knew at all [*Edward Garnett*, p. 47].

Under Garnett's direction, O'Flaherty was sent back to write about "seagulls and congers, a peasant's cow and the flight of a blackbird, and he at once produced sketches of the most delicate feeling and visual brilliance that few, even among the Irish, have equalled." In addition to setting aesthetic standards for O'Flaherty, Garnett introduced him to books that helped the young writer shape his Irish material—books by Dostoevsky, Gogol, Hemingway, and Joyce.

If Garnett was by far the most influential of O'Flahertys' friends, Dostoevsky, whose works were translated by Garnett's wife, Constance, had the most pervasive influence of any writer. After his first novel, O'Flaherty seems convinced that each novel should have a hero like those in Dostoevsky's works, a neoromantic figure embroiled in psychological traumas that cut him off from society. Although O'Flaherty admired Hemingway's work, he was not directly influenced by it; he had already mastered Gaelic rhythms and narrative simplicity in his first short stories, collected for publication in 1923.

For a short period, O'Flaherty sought a place among the Dublin *literati*. With one novel published, another to appear early in 1924, and with a book of short stories to his credit, some of which had been published in the *New Statesman* and in the *Spectator,* O'Flaherty came to Dublin as an established figure, a writer who had won his spurs without the help of Dublin literary men. At the time, of course, the Dublin scene was dominated by Yeats, A.E., and their followers. But some of the new men, notably, O'Flaherty, Austin Clarke, and F. R. Higgins, sought issues on which to attack their elders. O'Flaherty joined with the artist Cecil Salkeld and the poet and novelist Francis Stuart, in advancing a new creed in *To-morrow,* a journal memorable for the first appearance of Yeats's "Leda and the Swan," a poem that A.E. had refused to print in the *Irish Statesman.* In *To-morrow,* O'Flaherty published a short story, "The Red Petticoat," and it was there too that his second novel, *The Black Soul* received a laudatory review from L. K. Emery. So for a short period, at a key moment in his career, O'Flaherty could see himself as belonging to a "set."

In letters to the *Irish Statesman,* O'Flaherty and his friends opposed A.E.'s doctrine of nonviolence, praising a savagery that they thought necessary if a vital people were to acquire power and express itself. The young writers also opposed Yeats's control over Irish literary affairs. To strike at Yeats they censured Yeats's defense of O'Casey's *The Plough and the Stars,* saying that this play did not merit Yeats's esteem. Their stratagem apparently had little effect on Yeats, and it lost the young men the support of O'Casey, who had previously been sympathetic to the young writers. At the time O'Flaherty admired O'Casey as a spokesman for the working people, but O'Flaherty protested against O'Casey's use of Pearse's speeches in *The Plough and the Stars* as defamation of a national hero. In his autobiography O'Casey says that he was happy to separate himself from the cabal, adding that he thought that O'Flaherty had the arrogance of Yeats without the grace and goodwill of the poet.

The young writers lacked a core to their program; they had no tenets to champion after the demise of *To-morrow,* and they dwelled in a city that, as O'Flaherty said, had few resources to pay writers for their work. When O'Flaherty received no payment for his Irish play that was later translated as *Darkness,* he resolved to do no further writing for Gaelic groups. Yet in Dublin O'Flaherty assumed a role as one of the new realists, a position reflected in A.E.'s survey of the literary situation in Ireland in 1926: ". . . and now Sean O'Casey, James Joyce, and Liam O'Flaherty are winning for Ireland the repute of a realism more intimate, intense and daring than any other realism in contemporary literature." With the initiation of the Censorship Board in 1929, O'Flaherty joined other Irish writers in having their books banned in their own country. O'Flaherty, nevertheless, assisted in the formation of the Irish Academy of Letters in 1932 and was a charter member of this society, formed by Yeats mainly to combat censorship.

In 1927 O'Flaherty's scorn for Irish politics pervaded his only biography, a life of Tim Healy, the first governor-general of the Irish Free State, remembered chiefly as the betrayer of Parnell in Committee Room 15. This man was then a septuagenarian, one who was called "the Renegade" in some Irish circles. In his preface to the book, O'Flaherty warns his readers: "Let the whole book be read from the point of view of the merry and sometimes malicious imp that wrote it." In the book, O'Flaherty does not attempt a penetrating study of Healy or his character. Instead, he arranges the events of Healy's public life as milestones, adequately embedded in facts from other biographies, newspapers, and letters, so that these milestones and facts reveal the recurring venality of Irish politics. Since Healy was born in 1855, O'Flaherty lets his merry and malicious imp play upon ironies, chicaneries, and stupidities in Irish public life from 1855 to 1927.

Inevitably a study of Tim Healy turns on the contrast between Healy and Charles Stuart Parnell, a contest that to O'Flaherty was unequal from the start, for Parnell grew up with a code of honor and responsibility that was alien to Healy. Healy's guiding images, according to O'Flaherty, were the famine pits of Bantry, his birthplace in West Cork; Healy's father remarked that no one smiled during the three years of famine. As O'Flaherty sees it, Healy's abusive tongue grew out of his hatred against landlords, a hatred spilling over into all his other relationships. O'Flaherty, nevertheless, reveals Healy as an able parliamentarian, known for his wit and mastery of debate; he concludes that Healy voted against Parnell because he was convinced that Gladstone would withdraw his support from Home Rule if the Irish party retained Parnell as leader after the notorious divorce.

O'Flaherty indulges his merry and malicious imp in attacking Gladstone as a villain, a leader full of imperial deceit. His thesis is now considered untenable by historians. O'Flaherty is unsparing in his strikes against the Church, Gaelic enthusiasts, and new patriots: "Our patriots say that the national schools destroyed the remains of the Gaelic civilization and the Irish language. It is very doubtful if there ever was a Gaelic civilization of any consequence at the best of times . . . but the only civilization to which the Gaelic conquerors of this country seem to have been addicted was fighting, drunkenness, incest and chess playing" (p. 35).

If O'Flaherty was disenchanted with political life in the Irish Free State, he was equally disturbed by the rhetoric of the British Communists. After a visit of several months to the Soviet Union in 1930, he published an account of his travels in *I Went to Russia* (1931). Later in *Shame the Devil* he apologizes for a sportiveness in dealing with the Russian people, calling the book the most reprehensible thing he had ever done. Perhaps O'Flaherty was trying to shock some of the intellectual Communists in Britain. In several passages in *I Went to Russia* he scoffs at doctrinaire Communists, belittling those Russians who submerged their

humanity in a mechanical dedication to the rules of the
new government. His story of personal adventure in the
Soviet Union is unified by the brash, iconoclastic personality of the author. In almost every contact with
Russians, he tries to slice away stuffiness and jargon to
find the essential human being underneath. On board a
Soviet ship he becomes a comrade rather than an Irish
writer when the sailors learn that he has worked on
freighters. At the end of the book, O'Flaherty lists, in
all too rapid summary, his contact with the people
through his trips to the circus, zoo, racing meets, lemon-
ade kiosks, and hotel bars—trips made without a guide.
He played football with workmen; he rowed and swam
with them, queued up for cigarettes, and went to the
cinema, weddings, and funerals. He delighted in the
fact that the electric energies of the people, their crud-
ity, and their barbarism persisted despite the Revolution.

O'Flaherty's central insight into Communistic Russia
of 1930, as well as the governing language of the book,
is that Communism has become a religion for the people; it transforms their interior and exterior lives; in
fact Russia is the only country in the world where religion has influence. To him western Europe is effete,
a culture in which God is dead. In the end, O'Flaherty
is of two minds on the Soviet Union. He rejects the
dogmas that restrict humanity; he deplores the lockstep
scheduling of social enterprises, including the writing
of literature. But he admires the raw hope and dedication of people who build new cities; for a moment he
dreams of himself as one of their comrades, an adven-
turer helping them in their bold experiment. But he

admits that he is too cowardly to follow this dream, and he returns to the west.

While O'Flaherty rejoiced that the ordinary Russian retained his common humanity under a new government, he was indignant at the continued exploitation of the peasant in the Irish Free State. In a little book entitled *A Tourist's Guide to Ireland* (1930), he uses the format of a travel book to satirize priests and politicians, but his most incisive statements deal with the peasants. In the new Ireland the peasants are still victims of too many groups; everyone exploits them; no one really helps them. To him peasants are children; they are often brutish and they lack critical intelligence. Yet they have a quick sense of humor, they lack vulgarity, and they live in elemental harmony with nature: "The peasant responds to the seasons like a bird or beast. . . . He reproduces his kind methodically, without any concept of romantic love, and he dies practically without effort, since his imagination is not strong enough to torment him with visions."

O'Flaherty scorns patriots, sexless ascetics, and mystic loons, those Irishmen who hold the peasant to a mean, dull life and then talk to the outside world about these fine human beings midway between heaven and earth. As the worlds of business and industry intrude, the peasant, once a decent man, becomes shifty, dirty, hungry, fawning, and terrified of life and death. One type of peasant uses his cunning and lack of honor to rise in the world; he becomes a huckster, gombeen-man, priest, or politician. But O'Flaherty praises the peasant rebel: ". . . it is through the fiery eyes of these rebels that the Irish peasant must really be seen and not through his dirt, his hunger, his apathy and the helpless hands that he waves despairingly at the sky in which he sees no heaven of the blest." O'Flaherty admits that rebel peasants are rare, but he knows the type well—characters like Skerrett, O'Dwyer, his father, and, of course, himself.

Although O'Flaherty wrote many novels and short stories in the 1920s and 1930s, he was beset with recurring attacks of alcoholism, literary dryness, and despair. A prolonged period of despair and his successful efforts to recover his creative energies are the basis for his second autobiography, *Shame the Devil* (1934). At this time he was racked by family problems; apparently he was separated from his wife, Margaret Barrington, the former wife of Professor Edmund Curtis, a distinguished Irish historian at Trinity College. In *Shame the Devil* he speaks of his need to send money to his wife and daughter Pegeen, who was born in 1927. He wrote, "I have never taken pleasure in injuring a fellow human being, and yet my life has been strewn with the wreckage I have caused by my carelessness and folly." So intense was his depression that he considered suicide, speculating whether the ephemeral notoriety of his death would help the sale of his books for a year or two. In addition, he suffered from a mania to go into hiding, a malady afflicting him since the war.

In his flight from the British Isles he stopped first in Paris, where at a horse race he lost the money he had borrowed to pay for his recuperation. With the little money he had left, he went to Brittany, where he fell in with two fishermen, potential aristocrats of the new order, vigorous young Communists. They took O'Flaherty to their island, an outpost much like the Aran Islands. Among the simple fishing people he regained his literary voice and dashed off a story called "The Caress," which he printed along with the autobiography as evidence that he had emerged from melancholy and despair.

In *Shame the Devil,* O'Flaherty uses two voices to express the conflict between the artist and the man, a conflict that began, according to his account, when as a boy of nine he told a story to his mother. At that time he described the way that a man killed his wife so vividly that his mother went outside to warn the neighbors. When his mother, herself a skilled story teller, found her error, she reproved the boy so harshly that his delight in stories and fantasies had to go underground for many years. In his mature years, the *artist* and *man* continue a combat to which he had been accustomed since his youth. The *man* speaks for respectability, money, and esteem; the *artist* likes to be considered a rogue, a roisterer, and an enemy of society. Yet O'Flaherty realizes that the artist must have a discipline too, the discipline of "an ancient hermit scourging himself with a spiked thong." The artist also consoles himself with Edward Garnett's dictum, "To the artist, everything that exists justifies itself by the fact of its existence," a caution that kept him from propagandizing, probably his greatest temptation as an artist. The artist in O'Flaherty further fortifies himself by a belief in the necessity of struggle: "The degree of the individual human being's happiness is in direct ratio to the degree of his struggle against his environment." Man is superior to animals, he thought, because ". . . we are pre-eminent in our power to imagine a stage of perfection, which we call God and which we are trying to reach." Even if this goal is imaginary, he insists, it is worthwhile to believe in the delusion, our only defense against annihilation. In the novels O'Flaherty often uses crude, powerful figures impelled by a dream of perfection that is grossly inadequate for the crisis, but the dream is an embryonic expression of man's striving to reach perfection. At the conclusion of *Shame the Devil,* a book that contains his best passages on his childhood and his family, he feels that he has acquired control of himself, a control born out of desperation: "I have said good-bye to despair, since it cannot stay the swooping of the carrion crows."

O'Flaherty's life since 1934 is difficult to trace. His most recent novel is dated 1950, his most recent short story 1956. He has said that during World War II, from 1940 to 1947, he was marooned, spending time in Connecticut, the Caribbean, and South America. Since then he has traveled extensively, living in France and Ireland. In an interview on May 13, 1946, with a picture of him and his daughter Pegeen, O'Flaherty told a reporter from the *Irish Press* that he had spent most of the war years in a lonely house in Connecticut writing stories in English and Irish, emerging only occasionally to defend Irish neutrality in the war.

One of several unresolved problems in the life of O'Flaherty involves his attachment to Communism. Did O'Flaherty encounter personal or intellectual difficulties in dealing with Irish and British Communists? Did he abandon the party just as he broke away from the literary circles in Dublin? Was there so much of the rebel in O'Flaherty that he could not be doctrinaire about any movement? O'Flaherty's assignment to tour Russia in 1929 suggests that he had gained the approval of Communist leaders in England, but his covert attack on these leaders in *I Went to Russia* (1930) reveals his antagonism toward the leaders or toward the party itself. In addition, why are there not more pamphlets or articles attacking capitalism like the somewhat playful *A Cure for Unemployment* (1931)? A related issue is the absence of proletarian propaganda in O'Flaherty's novels and stories. In effect, did he subscribe almost immediately to the aesthetics of Edward Garnett, who insisted that pleas for social justice had no place in fiction? As a result of his study of the Marxist historians, did O'Flaherty develop his own theory on the evolution of human consciousness? Is this theory, evident especially in his novels, part of his disillusionment with Christianity and perhaps also with Communism? A study of the sources and gradual unfolding of O'Flaherty's view of human consciousness awaits the release of information from the author himself.

2
O'Flaherty as Novelist

As a young writer, O'Flaherty hoped that his novels would bring him fame. Perhaps his most significant disappointment as a writer was the limited response to *The Black Soul* (1924), his second novel, a story with numerous parallels to his own life and a book written under the guidance of Edward Garnett. Despite a wounded ego, O'Flaherty concentrated on writing novels for several years. In the period between 1923 and 1937 he published twelve novels, and he added two more to his list in 1946 and 1950. Yet he did not neglect the short story, for three collections were published between 1924 and 1929. For reasons which O'Flaherty himself might be pressed to explain, the novels differ from the short stories in regard to protagonists, plot, and the outlook of the narrator, but in both novel and short story he constantly searches for the means to dramatize man's primary instincts.

The novels of O'Flaherty have received only scattered attention in reviews and articles. However, there are a few good studies of the novels: William Troy's article in the *Bookman* in 1929, two doctoral dissertations, one by Anthony Canedo of the University of Washington, Seattle (1965), and the other by John N. Zneimer of the University of Wisconsin (1966), published in revised form as *The Literary Vision of Liam O'Flaherty* (1970). In a perceptive article (1966), Vivian Mercier praised *Famine* and *Skerrett* as O'Flaherty's most significant novels. In *Hibernia* (December 19, 1969) novelist John Broderick called O'Flaherty Ireland's greatest living writer. For many years O'Flaherty was classified with Joyce and O'Casey as a realist, although this label indicates chiefly a reaction to the writing of Yeats, Synge, and A.E. Yet O'Flaherty's novels still possess a depth and range that deserve reexamination. From the standpoint of literary history, O'Flaherty examines in his novels major shifts in the Irish psyche in the first half of the twentieth century; he describes in detail the effect of social and economic change on the peasant or country man; furthermore, his protagonists fit into significant psychological and existential patterns.

In general, O'Flaherty writes a realistic novel with readily recognized settings and characters, but the theme and plot revolve around a neoromantic protagonist. Although O'Flaherty has naturalistic leanings, he never makes the meticulous examination of environment of a Zola or Dreiser, in part because in his work environment does not control the protagonist. Instead, O'Flaherty's chief characters, often driven by obsessions, plunge into disaster. At times these protagonists have a Nietzschean will, but they are generally limited in intellect and judgment. As a group, O'Flaherty's novels deal with the dominant images affecting modern Ireland. As a novelist, he carries out a role that John Wain defines for the modern artist in *Sprightly Running:*

> I have said that people live according to their mental pictures. . . . And where do the mental pictures come from? There is no one simple answer, but I believe that the most powerful and widespread mental pictures, those which dominate the thought and action of a whole epoch, can usually be traced to the work of a few men, the supreme artists, the imaginative creators of their time. . . . There, at that centre, are artists who really form the consciousness of their time; they respond deeply, intuitively, to what is happening, what has happened and what will happen, and their response is expressed in metaphor and symbol, in image and fable. To be one of that band, to inhabit that creative centre, is the ambition of every author who has still not sold out.

Historically, O'Flaherty's novels study the Irish psyche from the famine of 1846–47, through the land war of the 1870s, through the revolution of 1916–23, and into the new Irish Free State that was struggling to establish its own social and political forms. But generally O'Flaherty does not attempt to depict historical attitudes with precision; with some exceptions, his peasants, rebels, landlords, priests, and shopkeepers speak for similar values, whether in the 1840s or the 1920s.

For the sake of discussion, O'Flaherty's novels may be divided into three groups: novels such as *Skerrett* that stress the roots of the Irish psyche, novels that deal with the Irish revolution of 1916–23, and novels that deal with the psyche of the new Ireland. This division has a convenience of setting and subject matter. In each group he develops themes or dominant images that have captured individuals and lead them to a special fanati-

cism, destructive to themselves and others. In his later
novels, he shifts from individual failures to an unexpected emphasis on the heights of the evolutionary
ladder, to types of men representative of the upper rung
of consciousness. Other approaches to the novel, of
course, repay examination. John Zneimer, for example,
organizes his book according to O'Flaherty's increasing
detachment from the central figures, his movement
from a personal involvement to an objective treatment
of his central figures. Yet in a brief survey, a division
according to setting and subject matter reveals O'Flaherty's persistent efforts to portray major movements
within the modern Irish psyche. In the discussion of the
historical novels, *Famine* (1937) and *Land* (1946) will
be treated before *Skerrett* (1932), largely because the
great famine and the Land League wars helped in mold-
ing a protagonist like Skerrett. *Skerrett* will be studied
in considerable detail because it exemplifies O'Flaherty's
control over the formal aspects of the novel.

In three novels O'Flaherty employs historical settings,
carefully selecting episodes from the past that have
altered Irish consciousness: the great famine, the Land
League Wars, and the transition from a peasant society
to one controlled by schools, government agencies, and
the Church. This process of social and cultural change
occurs throughout the nineteenth century in Ireland
as a whole, but O'Flaherty concentrates on the Aran
Islands and the west of Ireland where changes came late
and in a compressed form. Like other Irish writers,
O'Flaherty considers the famine a watershed between
an old and a new Irish mentality. Unlike most Irish
writers, however, O'Flaherty regards Parnell's Land

League rather than O'Connell's Association as the beginning of the Irish nation. As a native of Aranmore, O'Flaherty and his family exemplify the shift from an almost medieval world into that of the nineteenth and twentieth centuries. O'Flaherty could easily draw upon his own life and that of his parents and other islanders in presenting a social revolution that in many ways was more momentous for the peasant than the political struggle of 1916–23.

In one of Ireland's few popular novels, *Famine* (1937), O'Flaherty takes up tales of his childhood, when the famine was alive in folklore, to write a competent, lucid novel. But in many ways O'Flaherty is hampered by the mythology of the famine; he finds no means to break away from it to infuse his characters with great passion. In other words, he writes a predictable novel about a historical catastrophe. But *Famine* also illustrates O'Flaherty's mature control over a variety of scenes and characters. The principal action of the book involves the complete removal of peasants from Black Valley, near Galway, by death, eviction, and emigration. Its ablest individuals, a young farmer turned rebel, his wife, and his son escape to America, suggesting that only by rebellion and emigration may Ireland escape the ravages of famine and misgovernment. This escape, with its promise for the future liberation of Ireland, diminishes the tragedy, for it shifts the reader's attention from the silence of the valley. In the final scene, however, O'Flaherty stresses this emptiness of the valley. Here old Brian Kilmartin, the father of the rebel who escapes, hobbles out to the paddock, using his spade as a cane. On a frosty morning he starts to dig a grave for his wife, who died in bed. The old man falls forward on the spade, his dog barks and rests on his dead master, the last human being in the valley. Although this scene stresses the utter hopelessness in Ireland, the rebel's flight to America offers hope and continuity.

As I have suggested, the main sweep of the novel is toward the final stillness of the valley, for the forces of famine, famine fever, and corruption in government cannot be resisted. But in the narration of events, O'Flaherty is by no means a determinist; the people are driven out because of their ignorance and superstition; they lean on frail reeds and have no understanding of the incapacity of government to relieve their hunger. One by one their illusions are cut away—through the loss of the potato crop, through the confused system of landholdings, through the debauchery of the landlord's agent, through the empty gestures of the local relief committee and of agents sent from England, and through the greed of the local shopkeeper, a former peasant himself. The peasants do not realize that the Quaker relief group will pass through the valley but once. Unfortunately, they try to outwit an eviction gang hired by the landlord's agent by taking their animals to the hills, but when the gang destroys one cottage, the peasants quickly bring the animals down from the hills and surrender them in lieu of rent. What is even more pathetic, the peasants have no comprehension of madness and famine fever.

Although O'Flaherty describes a wide group of characters associated with the famine, he centers his attention on the Kilmartin family who live in Black Valley.

When they depart through emigration and death, all is lost; the valley is empty. Rooted in peasant traditions, the Kilmartins envision life only in terms of the land. The aging grandfather, Brian, the old man who falls on his spade during the last scene, insists that he buy whiskey for a wake even though the family needs the money for food. His faith that bad years would be followed by good years is unshakable, but he shrewdly uses an illness to pass on the household moneybag to his son, Martin, so that he would not lose patriarchal dignity.

Those who survive are the youthful Martin Kilmartin and his new wife, Mary, the most resourceful individuals in the family. Martin becomes a rebel, O'Flaherty's typical man of action fighting against the landlord's agent and eventually against British forces. Mary is similarly resourceful and also beautiful, a natural aristocrat, a recurring type in his novels. Martin courageously attacks the landlord's drunken agent, and Mary ingeniously provides food for her family and relatives. On taking charge of the household after her husband receives the moneybag, Mary cleans the cottage, arousing the ire of Martin's mother, who thinks that peasants are predestined to live in dirt. Mary forces Thomas Hynes, a likeable sixty-year old wastrel, to bathe and to clean his clothes. Mary also forces the men to plant a vegetable garden to supplement potatoes, the first such garden in Black Valley. She shares her decreasing supply of food with relatives and neighbors; she thwarts the debased proposal of the landlord's agent that she receive ten pounds for allowing him to whip her, and she also helps her sister escape after the latter has been accused of consorting with the landlord's agent. Whatever the circumstances, Mary acts decisively to sustain her family. When all her own food is gone she even steals bacon when the shopkeeper is preoccupied with a rush of peasants asking for food.

In writing of the famine, O'Flaherty expands upon folklore that includes degraded landlord's agents and peasants with lips green from eating nettles. In many instances O'Flaherty hardly advances or deepens the popular images and memories; as a novelist he falls victim to the conventionalized myths. As John Kelleher wrote in the *Atlantic Monthly* in 1945, *Famine* elicited a response in Ireland where the people were prepared for it. Too few scenes in the novel, however, possess the momentum of that in which a luminous cloud descends upon the valley, carrying the blight:

> And then, as the people watched, the cloud began to move lazily down upon the Valley. It spread out on either side, lost its form and polluted the atmosphere, which became full of a whitish vapour, through which the sun's rays glistened; so that it seemed that a fine rain of tiny whitish particles of dust was gently falling from the sky. Gradually a sulphurous stench affected the senses of those who watched. It was like the smell of foul water in a sewer. Yet, there was no moisture and the stench left an arid feeling in the nostrils. Even the animals were affected by it. Dogs sat up on their haunches and howled. Not a bird was to be seen, although there had been flocks of crows and of starlings about on the previous day. Then, indeed, terror seized the people and a loud wailing broke out from the cabins, as the cloud overspread the whole Valley, shutting out the sun completely.

After the cloud blackens, Brian, the grandfather, pulls

out stalks that "snapped like rotten wood." The potatoes in the second year of the famine promised to be
plentiful, but after this second blight, "the wailing was
now general all over the Valley." Few sections of the
book are so well developed as the one on the approach
of the cloud, a chapter brimming with a sense of inevi-
tability that marks O'Flaherty's short stories.

The mythology of the famine furnished O'Flaherty
with typical characters like the priest, the peasants, and
ineffectual men of goodwill like the vicar of the Church
of Ireland. But many of these characters perform their
functions as peasant victims, dissolute aristocrats, and
timid gentry without acquiring intensity and distinc-
tiveness. Besides Thomsy Hynes, one of the few characters rising above a stereotype is Dr. Hynes, the son of a
shopkeeper who becomes a doctor, thereby entering the
gentry. But his father's peasant, shopkeeping background prevents Dr. Hynes from attaining full status;
he passively endures humiliations from the landlord's
agent; he rediscovers his attachment to the common
people through the beauty of Mary Kilmartin and the
rhetoric of a patriotic curate. Dr. Hynes finally rebels
against his father who let people starve rather than re-
duce a price for food that had been guaranteed by
government order. A tormented, vacillating man, Dr.
Hynes dies of famine fever after visiting a peasant hovel.

O'Flaherty produced in *Famine* a well-organized
novel that sympathetically treats the major disaster of
modern Ireland, but he lacks a profound vision of the
past; he does not pierce deeply into the weakness and
nobility of men overwhelmed by forces that they could

hardly begin to understand. In *Famine,* he depends too much on the pattern of myths already clustered around the event.

In *Land* (1946) O'Flaherty attempts a second epic novel, this time on the land war of the 1870s. In many ways he had opportunity for a more original attack on the Irish past than he had in *Famine,* for he had written in his biography of Tim Healy that the national mind was formed during the struggle for land tenure, a movement begun by Michael Davitt but later taken over by Parnell. O'Flaherty may have begun the novel with the Land League at the center of the story, but strong characters come to dominate the novel. In *Land* O'Flaherty tries for the first time to provide an explicit philosophic base for conflicts within the novel.

The philosophizing for the Land League is done by Raoul St. George, an Irishman returned from France as a freethinker. But for O'Flaherty a freethinker is one who adopts "a purely personal attitude towards ideas and the phenomena of life." St. George, a landlord reduced to a small holding, has been liberated by his experiences in France so that he sides with a peasant rebel, O'Dwyer, against the most aggressive of the landlords, Captain Butcher. Butcher has the taint of an *arriviste.* A former Berkshire yeoman, Butcher came to Ireland as a member of the Royal Irish Constabulary and in a depressed time became a landlord. In his new position he upholds the rights of the aristocracy and denounces industrialists and liberals who are ruining England. As might be expected from his name, Butcher is barbaric and cruel. Years before the action of the novel, Butcher inveigled the older O'Dwyer into committing a crime for which he was hanged. Butcher now tries to trap the young O'Dwyer, an ideal O'Flaherty rebel. But Butcher can no longer pack juries, so the crime must be a serious one. Eventually the people rise up against Butcher and isolate him by a new punishment devised by Raoul St. George—the boycott. Although Butcher kills O'Dwyer, he is himself killed by a policeman. But the rebel survives through his wife and their infant son.

In *Land* O'Flaherty uses a structure based on the achievement of soldier, monk, and poet as the epitome of mankind on the evolutionary ladder, for they demonstrate the fullness of men in action, contemplation, and imagination, men who seek the unattainable. In *Land* the priest has been defrocked for taking arms from his dying brother during the Fenian uprising of 1867. He lives with a shopkeeper for years, but when the shopkeeper, an informer, is punished by a boycott and goes mad, the priest retires to a hermitage. The priest condemns St. George's boycott as an inhumane punishment, but he leaves the hermitage only when he is needed in a local rebellion of the Land League. The soldier in *Land,* O'Dwyer, burns with revenge because of the death of his father. Significantly, the chief moment of exaltation for O'Dwyer is in taking the Fenian oath. But O'Dwyer is a guerrilla leader, not a spokesman for the people. The third figure, the thinker, St. George, foresees the time when the peasants will control their own land; he invents the boycott and serves temporarily as leader of the people. If the action of the three leaders can be taken as a standard, O'Flaherty focuses on an individual's aspirations and the convergence of temperament and idealism that makes a soldier, monk, or poet rather than an average, sensual man.

All three figures, however, express a part of their aspirations by finding delight and beauty in danger, The rebel O'Dwyer, who had been in America as a young man, sees beauty only in danger; for him, "Cape Horn was beautiful simply because his ship almost foundered there." Lettice, St. George's daughter who marries O'Dwyer, shares this joy in danger. On the honeymoon Lettice is tied to the stern of a small boat for six hours during a storm: "At once I felt a greater joy than I had ever known before." At the end of the novel, despite the death of her husband, Lettice discovers another kind of joy: "Her ecstasy of motherhood, now coming to a climax, had already conquered the bitterness of her tragedy. There was only rapture in her eyes." O'Flaherty also stresses the short-lived excitement of the people as they engage in combat with the British troops in defending their land.

Land is limited like other O'Flaherty novels by the author's inadequate hold on inner and outer rings of characters. One circle does not reinforce the other. Although he points a way toward the genesis of the Irish nation in his example of the Land League wars, he does not succeed in merging people and leaders. The local campaign does not take on the significance of the Easter Rising of 1916. The rebel's actions are those of an isolated guerrilla leader and do not flow out of the thought of Raoul St. George, a rather stilted figure, and the priest remains at the fringe of the action, a noble though uninfluential leader. While some of the tales of the peasants fit into the traditions of the Land League

and its struggle, they hardly reflect an awakened national awareness based on ancestral memories and a
deep attachment to the soil. In some ways, O'Flaherty's
treatment of the Easter Rising in *Insurrection* completes themes and motifs of *Land,* just as *The Black
Soul* completes many conflicts initiated in *Thy Neighbour's Wife.*

Published in 1932, O'Flaherty's ninth novel, *Skerrett*
is one of his best integrated works, the equal of *The
Black Soul.* In *Skerrett* O'Flaherty returns to the Aran
Islands for the first time since *The Black Soul* (1924),
this time to write about a schoolmaster similar to one
O'Flaherty knew as a youth. In some ways, *Skerrett* extends the setting and theme of *The Black Soul,* for both
books with an Aran scene deal with a feverish, depressed
man who is so battered by circumstances that he is
forced to discover his own integrity and independence.
But the differences in the quest of the protagonist speak
eloquently of the change in O'Flaherty over an eight-
year period. *The Black Soul* was published when O'Flaherty was twenty-eight; *Skerrett* when he was thirty-six.
In *The Black Soul* he was at the beginning of his career
and seemed totally absorbed in a year's crisis of a young
man at the edge of sanity after war injuries and world
travel. But in *Skerrett* he deals with fifteen years in the
life of a schoolmaster suffering from melancholia and
despair, a man who wins a sense of personal freedom
only after his strength and possession have been stripped
from him. In addition, the two novels differ markedly
in their approach to the islanders. In *The Black Soul,*
the peasants possess the traits of a permanent peasantry;
they live embedded in traditions that defy time and

generations. In *Skerrett* the peasants' traditional ways
are in the process of breaking up by the forces of business and government; the values of generations are
exposed to changes that bring prosperity to some and
heartbreak to others.

A minor though telling clue to Skerrett's struggle
toward individual independence lies in O'Flaherty's
allusions to Ibsen. He repeats the phrase "an enemy of
the people" to refer to Skerrett, the schoolmaster. Although Skerrett lacks the sophistication and singular
dedication of Ibsen's Dr. Stockmann, he possesses Stockmann's sturdy persistence in seeking justice for the
people. O'Flaherty's Skerrett is blunt, uncouth, erratic,
impulsive, a man with an inchoate psyche, groping
toward shifting lights, a man unable to cope with his
own blindness and arrogance. Skerrett's entire effort is
to arrive at the resolution and independence that Dr.
Stockmann has at the start of Ibsen's play. A second
allusion to Ibsen concerns the island doctor, Dr. Melia,
an anarchist who keeps a wild duck. To Skerrett, Dr.
Melia espouses not only anarchy but individuality and
cooperatives. He finally runs off with a young daughter
of the landlord, thus adding to Skerrett's isolation.

In the fifteen years of action of *Skerrett*, 1887–1902,
the protagonist serves the islanders not only as schoolmaster but also as a spokesman for the traditional values
and wisdom of the peasants. Despite Skerrett's help, the
peasants' mode of living is seriously altered by the construction of a pier, by subsidies for trawlers, by the
creation of new offices, and by grants to islanders in the
favor of authorities, especially the parish priest, and by
the greatly increased use of money. Economic change

precipitates social change, but in O'Flaherty's novel the most significant change occurs within Skerrett.

When Skerrett comes to Nara, an anagram for Aran, he is a depressed schoolmaster, driven from his previous post on the mainland; he had broken the jaw of a man who objected to his rough treatment of his son. Skerrett himself wanted to emigrate to America, but his ordinarily passive wife objected and used her influence with the island priest to have Skerrett appointed schoolmaster. The previous schoolmaster had gone mad after five years on the island. Thus Skerrett begins his work, an embittered man, determined to impose the English language and values upon his scholars.

Skerrett seems transformed when his son is born; he enlarges his world almost immediately. He reconciles himself to his wife; he learns Irish and teaches it at school, becoming an authority on Gaelic matters. In his school he changes from a severe though effective taskmaster to an inspired teacher. At the same time, Skerrett takes up religious exercises and makes the old pilgrimages of Aran. He finds a new confidant in whom he has complete trust, Father Moclair, the parish priest.

The next stage is marked by Skerrett's descent into disillusionment and despair, his physical and mental disintegration. This stage, incidentally, consumes about two-thirds of the book, a flaw inasmuch as O'Flaherty does not adequately dramatize the events of the earlier stages; he relies too much on summary when he should create scenes to emphasize the changes in Skerrett. But O'Flaherty presents the disintegration of Skerrett with consummate skill. Skerrett's physical and mental breakdown have at least two external causes—his wife and

Father Moclair—but they also stem from his own incapacity to judge himself and others. But the turning
point in Skerrett's new life is the accidental death of his
seven-year-old son. After the funeral, his wife resents
Skerrett's offer that they live out their days in peace because of their common loss; she refuses and turns to
alcohol. One day as Skerrett enters the house, she
swings the tongs at his head, giving him a blow that
initiates severe headaches. Eventually his wife, also a
teacher, is dismissed by the visiting inspector because of
her secret drinking; she goes mad and is taken to an
asylum on the mainland. Although he is rid of his wife,
Skerrett cannot remarry, an additional cause of depression. But Skerrett's new enemy, Father Moclair, ha-
rasses him at every turn. His revulsion toward the priest
began on the day of the boy's funeral when the priest
insisted that a poor man leave some coins after Skerrett
urged the peasant to make no offering at all. Skerrett
gradually loses command of himself and of his work at
school. He becomes slovenly, unaware of the changes in
himself. Finally, his lack of control becomes public at a
confirmation exercise when his pupils are examined by
an administrator for the bishop. Skerrett's pupils are
hopeless, even with the books in their hands. At this
gathering outside the church, Skerrett, embarrassed and
irritated, argues vehemently with Father Moclair. The
priest strikes him with his stick, on the same spot his
wife had used the tongs. Skerrett's only refuge is Dr.
Melia, the philosophical anarchist who advocates an
economy based on cooperation and love.

   After the blow by Father Moclair, Skerrett's decline is
rapid. He is driven from his position and from the

schoolmaster's house, retreating to a cottage he had built in a remote village. Even here he is only tolerated, for the people fear the priest's order to boycott Skerrett. Raging, Skerrett walks to the main village to strike Father Moclair, but a partisan of the priest gives Skerrett another blow that touches off a fit of madness. Skerrett is taken to an asylum where he dies within six months. But Skerrett is remembered in Nara; he becomes legendary as a man who stood up for his beliefs and defied authority; he was his own man even when rejected by all the people.

Skerrett is driven to an untimely ruin by his wife and by the leader of society in Nara, Father Moclair. But O'Flaherty presents the wife and priest as overwhelming destructive types rather than as individualized characters; hence they seem a part of Skerrett's fate; they are large, almost impersonal forces bent on his ruin. Father Moclair resembles a Machiavellian entrepreneur, as he attempts to import the benefits of an industrial age into the peasant community. During the fifteen years of the action, the priest increases in girth, pride, and greed, and he gradually makes the islanders subservient to him.

As suggested previously, *Skerrett* is remarkable among O'Flaherty's novels for integrating a society into the story of the protagonist. Like Skerrett's life, the islanders suffer numerous disruptions from external change. They are carried into a new era, seemingly through the craftiness of the priest who controls the District Council. The traditional ways of the islanders are protected only by confused agents, Skerrett, Dr. Melia, the anarchist, and a few of the older islanders.

In the few peasants singled out for description and action, O'Flaherty concentrates on shifting social and economic conditions. At the start of the novel, Coonan, a newly appointed rate-collector, has started his ascent from peasantry. On board the hooker that brings Skerrett to Nara, Coonan treats the natives as Skerrett treats Coonan, as a social inferior. Coonan dresses in shop clothes, a swallow-tailed coat, trousers, boots, and cravat, while the natives continue to wear rawhide shoes, blue frieze waistcoats, dark blue frieze shirts, and wide-brimmed black hats. Coonan tells the peasants: " 'It's English gave me bacon of a Sunday morning for my breakfast and gives me tea twice a day, while ye are all living on Indian meal porridge and potatoes and salt fish.' "

Yet other peasants, particularly the older ones, are frustrated by the changes. One of the most eloquent of these is the island wit, a character also used in *Thy Neighbour's Wife,* Grealish. Now an old man, Grealish earned his title of island wit by deceiving an English foreman on a construction job, but Grealish also had to bear the scrutiny of the islanders for some time before they allowed an unknown, barefoot urchin to sit in Mulligan's public house with a circle of men who would buy him an unlimited number of pints of stout. Grealish was called "the smartest man," in part because he supported a family of twelve girls without working hard. In *Skerrett,* Grealish's comments abruptly conclude the questioning period for confirmation. When the bishop's administrator asks about God's omniscience, Grealish answers, " 'Well! Then as He knows everything, what's the need for this little breeches of a bishop's mate putting us under an examination? Doesn't God know well that we're ignorant people and that we know nothing, so what's the good of asking us?' " In the voice of the wise fool, Grealish concludes with a Wordsworthian speech on the ingrained reverence islanders have for nature and for the Lord of creation. Grealish's eloquence rounds out a defense of the peasants that the irascible Skerrett would be unable to make.

In *Skerrett* O'Flaherty follows an unusual pattern for showing the changes within the protagonist. As pointed out, Skerrett, a surly, embittered man, discovers a vision of life that is soon shattered. He is crowded into despair by internal and external forces, but out of the despair he attains a sense of personal freedom just before he becomes insane and dies. The discovery of freedom on the far side of despair has become a familiar formula since the existentialism of Sartre, but O'Flaherty employs this pattern long before it became common in fiction. Skerrett is abandoned by everyone; his wife is in an asylum; he himself is proscribed; his last friend, the doctor, flees with the landlord's daughter. But Skerrett reaches a peak on the evolutionary scale, embodying, though crudely, man's will to power, beauty, and immortality. However, Skerrett's decline and renewal is not a typical pattern in O'Flaherty's novels. Often the narrator begins with a protagonist trapped in an obsession. He commits a crime or prepares for an extravagant deed; gradually the protagonist grasps the simplicity of his attack on life. O'Flaherty employs a variety of recognition scenes to fit character and circumstance. The voluptuary Gilhooley peers into the void after he has committed a murder; the Stranger in *The Black Soul* discovers an elemental harmony with nature as he escapes the bonds of despair; Gypo Nolan in *The Informer* dimly perceives the evil in his betrayal and asks for forgiveness; the young recruit in *Insurrection* rushes to his death, completely satisfied that his destiny lies in sacrificing his life for Ireland. At times O'Flaherty closes a novel with the hope for the future resting on a child or in escape to America, or he may conclude with the negation of hope. In *The House Of Gold*, for example, a provincial town is doomed to further dullness as the leading men of the town are killed or immobilized. In all these struggles O'Flaherty resorts to melodrama, his literary means for showing the eruptions of passion and for exposing instinctual forces that cannot be reconciled within an individual. For O'Flaherty melodrama has become a symbol of the modern fury that sunders the bond of order in the individual and in society.

In his fourteen novels O'Flaherty does not experiment with the role of the narrator. Despite his friendship with Edward Garnett, O'Flaherty seems untouched by the work of Henry James and Conrad. Almost always O'Flaherty's narrator is the classic third person omniscient narrator, a *persona* excited by strong protagonists and unusual events. As an observer of modern man, he attends closely to the instinctive and passionate reactions; he is sensitive to man's crippling obsessions and alert to man's tendency to blunder into nets from which he cannot extricate himself. But his narrator seldom shirks his duties as storyteller; he advances the narration rapidly; he idles only briefly, if at all, for com-

ment; he avoids with a clean narrative outline the
bypaths of reminiscence or speculation. While the
narrator generally explores sympathetically only the
protagonist, he rests with a common-sense view of the
conflicts within secondary figures. Despite his well-
established views on Communism and the Church, he
seldom promotes Marxism or anticlericalism in his
novels. On occasion he develops a scene at two levels,
mainly to show the confused mind of a protagonist. In
Thy Neighbour's Wife, for example, Father McMahon
listens to the simple confessions of the peasants as he
torments himself with doubts about the teachings of the
Church; in *The Puritan* Francis Ferriter similarly tries
to explain a murder he has committed to a priest as he
relives in memory a host of associations with his sup-
pressed love for the whore whom he killed.

O'Flaherty avoids poetic devices in his prose, although an occasional epic simile recalls his training in
the classics. So intent is O'Flaherty on raw experience
that he emphasizes man's suffering and turmoil at the
expense of precision of expression. At times the narrator
rushes along, dropping clichés, awkward phrases, and
sentences that ring hollow. Frequently he fails to exploit ironies inherent in the situation of the protagonist.
Whether the narrator's directness derives from de Maupassant, the Gaelic storytellers, or other influences, he
respects the visible, physical world. His narrator is consumed with the necessity for sketching the immediate
situation and laying bare at once the feelings of the
characters. The reader is never in doubt about external
circumstances. In *Skerrett* the author introduces in the
first sentence the new life awaiting the schooling master:

"On a wild day in February, 1887, the hooker Carra Lass brought David and his wife from Galway to the island of Nara."

A serious flaw in O'Flaherty's novels is his frequent failure to distinguish between scene and summary, between drama and exposition—that is, he lacks the gift of the skilled novelist to select and treat background expeditiously and to concentrate on the development of simple or complex scenes. In *Skerrett,* for instance, the author leaves many scenes half-developed or only touched upon, even though they could intensify the opposition between Skerrett and his wife or between Skerrett and Father Moclair. The narrator skims over Skerrett's achievements; he never shows him at his height even though he states that Skerrett made great changes within himself after the birth of his son. He does not show Skerrett with his son, thus leaving the reader unprepared for the impact of the son's death on the father. O'Flaherty's consummate skill in the stories of sketching in people and places often fails him in the novels where the context requires extended dramatization.

As a novelist, O'Flaherty has weaknesses in vision and technique that prevent his work from attracting widespread attention, but in works like *The Black Soul* and *Skerrett* he treats problems of the modern temper with a raw vitality appropriate to the experience of his protagonists. O'Flaherty must be accounted a perceptive observer of the dominant images of his countrymen and of western man. He probes the void, the emptiness of men whose faith has been broken, whose imaginations have been twisted by the social, political, or economic demands of the age. Often brusque in presentation, O'Flaherty nevertheless pursues the unassimilated experience of modern life, projecting it in novels that have been too readily neglected by critics and ordinary readers.

3

The War Novels

Despite O'Flaherty's reputation as the novelist of the Irish Revolution, only two of his fourteen novels have settings during the period of 1916–23: *The Martyr* (1923) and *Insurrection* (1950). Two other novels, however, may be included in a group of war novels, *The Informer* (1925) and *The Assassin* (1928), for *The Informer* deals with gunmen and a revolutionary cell, and *The Assassin* studies the split mentality of a gunman, though in a postwar period. In dramatizing man's recourse to violence O'Flaherty preferred the small intense world of Ireland to the larger world he knew from military service and travel. Somehow his love-hate relation to Ireland fired his imagination. But despite his Irish settings O'Flaherty is a close student of the modern temper. In *The Informer*, Gypo Nolan develops a rudimentary sense of identity only after betraying his only friend; the gunman in *The Assassin* struggles with a divided personality, which he discovers only after he resolves to kill a political leader; the protagonist in *The Martyr* is cemented in a noble idealism when an armed attack demands decisive action; and finally in *Insurrection* three special types of men on the evolutionary scale—soldier, monk, and poet—help to bring an Irish dream of centuries to fruition during the Easter Rising of 1916.

Even a brief discussion of O'Flaherty's war novels, however, should include comment on *The Return of the Brute* (1929). This crudely and evidently hastily written novel hardly rises above a conventional protest against the horror of trench warfare. In *The Return of the Brute,* O'Flaherty reinforces his theme with repeated references to the bestiality of man. For example, in the climactic scene between the hero, Gunn, and the corporal, Gunn is about to strangle a regulation-mad corporal. The author remarks, "It was a struggle between two brutes, and Gunn was the superior brute." In this story, nine men go over the top on the night of March 20, 1917; they are wiped out without firing a shot as they blindly follow their corporal, each man touching the man ahead. During the attack, they lose all sense of discipline as they are ordered to dig holes in frozen earth. Just as they settle in one spot, they are ordered to advance. Horror is heaped on horror. In the dark, one man cries, " 'Whew! I just stuck my hands into somebody's rotten guts. God! What a stink!' " Eight of the nine men die; one is shot six times through the stomach; another drowns in mud; a cowardly youth dies of fright; Gunn and the corporal fight and Gunn kills one of his comrades by throwing a grenade in a hole where the corporal was supposed to be. Chaos and brutality prevail as the narrator races on in a single key on the bestiality of modern war.

The Return of the Brute, however, is a sport among O'Flaherty's novels, for it is set outside of Ireland, it lacks a commanding figure with a complex psychology, and the action is limited to horrifying incidents. But in *The Informer* (1925), O'Flaherty studies a brute of a man who discovers himself as a person only after he learns that he has committed the worst of Irish sins, informing on a comrade. Curiously, O'Flaherty deprecates his best-known work, for in *Shame the Devil* he claims that he wrote *The Informer*

> . . . determined that it should be a sort of highbrow detective story and its style based on the technique of the cinema. It should have all the appearance of a realistic novel and yet the material should have hardly any connection with real life. I would treat my readers as a mob orator treats his audience and toy with their emotions, making them finally pity a character whom they began by considering a monster.

In 1934 he may have aimed this barb at critics who praised *The Informer* and neglected *The Black Soul.* But in a letter to Edward Garnett on September 18, 1924, quoted by John Zneimer (*Literary Vision of Liam O'Flaherty,* p. 69), O'Flaherty lays out the principal movements of the novel and describes a style appropriate to each movement. He planned to begin with a brutal style to conform to the grossness of Gypo Nolan's mind; he was to shift to a sympathetic note as Gypo begins to sense his own identity under the pressure of inquiry and imprisonment; then he planned to change to a rapid, abandoned narrative as Gypo is cornered by his enemies, and to finish with pity as members of the Revolutionary Cell shoot Gypo. But the reader of the novel cannot detect the distinctions described in the letter, for the author plunges forward in a nervous, energetic fashion, completely absorbed in advancing the action.

In 1925 O'Flaherty may have intended in *The Informer* to indict outlawed clusters of the Irish Republican Army (I.R.A.) that continually disrupted public meetings; at the same time he was probably aiming his arrows at Communist cells in Britain. As O'Flaherty himself said, *The Informer* reveals no secrets of the I.R.A., and the cell is called simply the *revolutionary group,* as if O'Flaherty desired to write about a rudimentary person in any small revolutionary group. But the novel's emphasis falls on the upward movement of Gypo Nolan's consciousness.

A man of brute strength, a former Dublin policeman, Gypo Nolan acts as a revolutionary only through the quick mind of his friend Frankie McPhillip. Together they make an effective team, but Gypo and Frankie are expelled from the cell when they become drunk on assignment and McPhillip shoots and kills the secretary of a farmers' union. When McPhillip flees to the Dublin hills, Gypo wanders the slums of Dublin, penniless and befriended only by a prostitute, Connemara Maggie. Out of desperation Gypo painfully decides to inform on McPhillip, who is dying of consumption and exposure— in order to receive the reward of twenty pounds. As Gypo emerges from the police barracks with the money, he is puzzled by a strange feeling, but as yet he has no sense of guilt.

Through betraying his friend and protector, Gypo begins his slow discovery of evil and of himself. The bulk of the story deals with Gypo's spending of the reward, his betrayal by a whore who befriended him when he was without money, his visit to the parents of the man he informed on, and a harrowing inquest by the revolutionary leader and men. When Gypo breaks down, "his whole body shivered and started into awe-inspiring movement, monstrous and inhuman, revolting as a spectacle of degrading vice and yet pitiful in its helplessness." Even the hardened revolutionaries, except for Gallagher, the leader, are stirred: "They only knew at that moment, that he was a poor, weak human being like themselves, a human soul, weak and helpless in suffering, shivering in the toils of the eternal struggle of the human soul with pain." Imprisoned, Gypo gathers his vast strength, breaks out of his crude cell, and runs wildly through the streets. But he is pursued by Gallagher's men, who fear that Gypo would reveal their secrets to the police. Wounded and dying, Gypo finds McPhillip's mother in church, asks her forgiveness, and dies on the church floor, his arms outspread.

O'Flaherty succeeds in gradually unfolding the dim awareness of a human being emerging into the light of consciousness, only to find himself guilty of the most heinous offense, of betraying the one person necessary to his existence. Only through acute physical and mental suffering does Gypo rise above the level of an animal. Unfortunately, the dialectic that O'Flaherty might have developed between Gypo Nolan and Dan Gallagher never materializes. At this stage in the novels, O'Flaherty develops only a single strong figure. Gallagher has cosmic aspirations, but he is cruel, fascistic, and unduly fearful of Gypo. Gallagher claims: "Civilization is a process in the development of the human species. I am an atom of the human species, groping in advance, impelled by a force over which neither I nor the human species have any control." Gallagher has the language of a Nietzschean superman, but he uses it mainly as a cover for cruelty. By failing to exploit the differences between Gypo's emerging consciousness and Gallagher's cosmic views, O'Flaherty ignores many contrasts and ironies implicit in the relationship between the two men.

After *The Informer,* O'Flaherty leaves the Gypo Nolans and turns to the Dan Gallaghers, men with self-transcending obsessions that lead them to violence. In *The Assassin* a gunman continues to act out of the code of ambush and secret attack that was honored during the Revolution. Written in 1928, *The Assassin* follows perilously close to the details of the murder of Kevin O'Higgins in 1927. O'Higgins was a strong, energetic leader of the Free State, a man much admired by W. B. Yeats. In his own mind, O'Flaherty's assassin shoulders a lonely, heroic role, but he discovers in himself a dual personality, with masculine and feminine elements vying for mastery:

> One was terror-stricken, eagerly watching for enemies, acutely conscious of the most minute details of life, smelling, looking, listening, reacting to every touch in an abandoned manner . . . [it] was feverishly busy marshalling thoughts and impressions covering the whole expanse of existence . . . it had a feminine attribute, because it was negative, hysterical and cunning, preying on his other personality, just as a woman preys on her mate.
> The other, new-born personality was masculine, a scoffing, arrogant, contemptuous one. With a bold, callous

will, it caught and crushed every idea and suggestion that was offered to it, rummaged through it, plundered what was useful and cast out the remainder. This personality existed in his body like a foreigner. It despised his body [p. 50].

McDara oscillates between fear and cosmic aspiration on one side and strong determination and desire for independence on the other side, but after plotting the murder he never finds an equilibrium. At the start of his plot to kill the minister, McDara knows briefly, "the furious ecstasy of assassination. In this state he felt possessed of such power that he had merely to will a thing and it should be done." The assassin tries to justify the murder: " 'In the first place, our business is not to cripple England but to create a superior type of human being here.' " But as he vacillates McDara wants no power for himself, for he feels that the superior man is so rare that he should not accept public office lest he be corrupted. In his masculine moments, he renews his determination by saying that through him the people are making a gesture of defiance against tyranny. In the coming order, he believes, the people must trample on everything, including God. Here and elsewhere O'Flaherty advances Nietzsche's theme on the death of God, an expression of the archindividualism of the masculine side of McDara and an ominous warning of the chaos of a godless social order.

In carrying out his plot against the government minister, McDara is thorough, ruthless, and unbending, yet a sense of disillusionment, his unrecognized *anima,* vexes him. Instead of discovering a new revelation from the assassination, he feels that he is a man caught in a dirty room in a slum: "I am going to do something which has no meaning and is simply a waste of energy. I know that and yet I am going to do it, although it means nothing and it will have no effect." Curiously, McDara finds a bond between himself and the victim, but he soon feels that even though he and the victim may become part of a single whole, only the superior part will survive. As the group of assassins pump bullets into the body of the minister as he walks to Mass on Sunday, McDara is ecstatic. Only afterward when Mc-Dara hears people talk in the street does he realize that he is not a liberator but a murderer. In his dazed wanderings in Dublin, he buys a dinner for a man ironically called Lawless. Famished from several days with little food, Lawless tells McDara: " 'I mean there's no moral justification as far as I am concerned . . . for unconsidered action.' " As McDara escapes to England, he is awakened on the train by a ticket taker; a glimmer of the evil in men wells up in him, and he involuntarily utters, " 'Christ died for us all, didn't he?' " All he knows is that he is going to London to meet Kitty Mellett and to kill himself afterward. Through McDara, O'Flaherty makes an extended study of an isolated self, unable to balance fear and desire for independence, caught in the vise of dominant images formed when a violent single killing is extolled as a heroic blow for his country.

One of O'Flaherty's innovations in respect to Irish characters is Brian Crosbie in *The Martyr* (1933), a story of the Irish Civil War of 1922–23. Perhaps only in the setting of the confused guerrilla warfare could O'Flaherty make plausible a passive figure like Crosbie, the commander of a Republican unit. The martyr becomes commander of a garrison in a small village in County Kerry mainly through the national reputation that he has gained for a thirty-two day hunger strike against the British. But in *The Martyr* O'Flaherty forces decision and action upon his passive protagonist. When the Free State troops approach the village, Crosbie, a man of contemplation, scorns action, saying, "Prayer and contemplation and suffering are what appear to me most capable of purifying the souls of our people, and of making our country free and noble." Because he is convinced that pagan England is corrupt and that England has corrupted Ireland, he asserts that "the soul of the nation must be purified through suffering." Crosbie envisions a Gaelic Catholic Ireland, a revival of the land of the saints and scholars that will again preserve religion for all of Europe.

Fiction about martyrs, however, runs high risks, for the protagonist generally retreats into the background; in addition, O'Flaherty succumbs too to the attractiveness of his own creations, the antagonists to Crosbie. These include a lean, hardened rebel, Tracy, a beautiful woman leader of the Republicans, and a brutal imaginative torturer, Tyson. But Crosbie himself is hardly a heroic martyr; rather he is a martyr *manqué*. Crosbie resorts to the lofty rhetoric of contemplation about when a commander should lead his men. Perhaps O'Flaherty finds the respect for passive suffering too great in Ireland; he suggests that the rhetoric of stoic endurance, demonstrated in numerous hunger strikes, paralyzes an individual who resorts to it instead of taking immediate action.

O'Flaherty plays upon the ambiguities in Tyson, an unofficial torturer of the Irish Free State, a man whom the new officials cannot praise but also a man whom they cannot do without in their campaign to wipe out die-hard Republicans. Tyson uses a Nietzschean rhetoric to persuade Crosbie to accept the authority of the Free State; he holds that the day of the martyr is past, that he himself wants to murder martyrdom. He tells Crosbie, " 'I am killing you in cold blood. That's what we must learn to do in Ireland. To kill in cold blood whoever stands in the way of our progress. To own no God above the state.' " Unarmed, Tyson leads Crosbie up a mountain to crucify him, but Crosbie makes no effort to escape, so strong is his view that suffering in itself is a positive virtue. But O'Flaherty's reenactment of the crucifixion is embarrassing and quixotic; he raises more implications about suffering, redemption, and atonement than he can begin to develop adequately. When the burning cross to which Crosbie is tied falls from a cliff, it is seen at a distance by Tracy's girl's friend, who comments to the wounded Tracy, " 'It's only a rabbit caught by a weasel,' " a metaphor O'Flaherty uses to deprecate the passivity of Crosbie and the cruelty of Tyson and to show the contrast between an arrogant self and one lost in sentimentality.

O'Flaherty surrounds Crosbie with energetic, colorful figures that emphasize the absurdity of Crosbie's clinging to the ideals of a martyr. The rebel Tracy follows the pattern of O'Flaherty's typical rebel; he is reckless, decisive, quick to intercept the intelligence of the Free-Staters, and a worshiper of the new god of the machine. He is a committed socialist who happened to be in

Kerry when the Civil War began. Because of Crosbie's inaction, Tracy plans a raid on Free-State forces with himself as leader. In the skirmish, Tracy is badly wounded. Another antagonist in dramatizing the inertia of Crosbie is Angela Fitzgibbon, a romanticized version of Constance Markiewicz. She takes command when Crosbie should act against the troops coming into the town. Angela and Crosbie are taken prisoners, but the commandant of the Free-State troops, Colonel Hunt, would like to release them as part of his policy of mollifying churchmen and patriots. But Hunt, a *bon vivant* who was rewarded for his long service to the cause, cannot persuade Tyson to liberate Crosbie. As part of his scheme to win the leading men of the area to the Free-State government, Colonel Hunt sponsors a dinner, hoping to revive some of the elegance associated in this area only with the gentry. At this dinner a word from the parish priest would have saved Crosbie, but the priest, made comfortable by the wine, fears to disrupt the camaraderie created by Hunt's hospitality.

In *The Martyr* O'Flaherty organizes one of his penetrating studies of postrevolutionary Ireland and the confused values growing out of the achievement of the Tracys, Crosbies, and Angela Fitzgibbons. All of them are threatened by the appearance of a new figure on the landscape, Tyson, who along with Crosbie is an important addition to the cast of characters in Irish fiction.

In what seems to be O'Flaherty's final novel, *Insurrection* (1950), the author overlays his theory of mental evolution on the historical events of the Easter Rising of 1916. O'Flaherty may have several intentions in writing on a familiar subject at this time. In part he offers

an antidote to the cynicism setting in against the sacri-
fices made by an earlier generation; he also renders
accurately the combination of elation and fear of raw
recruits in the Irish Volunteers and the Irish Republican Army. But O'Flaherty's principal achievement in
Insurrection flows from the combined treatment of the
most intense period in modern Irish history with his
view that soldier, poet, and monk dramatize the heights
of human achievement—man's will to power, beauty,
and immortality, a division used in *Land* and other
works.

In *Insurrection,* the soldier, Bartley Madden, a
twenty-four-year-old farmer from Connemara, travels to
Liverpool to earn money so that he can buy a farm and
marry. On his return, he is robbed in Dublin, but on
Easter Monday, 1916, he hears Padraic Pearse read a
proclamation of the Irish Republic outside the General
Post Office. Somehow Madden absorbs the spirit although he does not understand Pearse's words. Madden
is further goaded into helping the Irish volunteers by
an old woman, a type of Kathleen ni Houlihan, who
wants Madden to protect her sixteen-year-old son who is
fighting in the General Post Office. But it is only when
Madden meets Thomas Kinsella, a soldier with the will
and resolution of the monk, that he finds his role as an
Irish revolutionary: "The vague mystical longings inspired in him by the poet's word had taken flesh, in this
lean man with an ascetic face and the mysterious eyes of
a monk. He felt taut from head to foot, like a drawn
bow, as he waited to establish contact with his chosen
one." Under Kinsella's tutelage, the *Idea,* O'Flaherty's
apt term for complete dedication to the cause of Irish

Republicanism, penetrates Madden's being. At first Madden is ecstatic as his platoon cuts down British soldiers as they march down a thoroughfare. In word and attitude, Madden emulates Kinsella. Finally, when Madden realizes that he must die, he tells Kinsella, " 'If it's God's will that I'm to die, let it be so.' " An ennobling fatalism of young men finding their destiny in death for Ireland runs through the novel, lending a calm dignity to O'Flaherty's story, a marked contrast to the bitter, nervous intensity of stories like *The Assassin* and *The Puritan*.

The soldier, monk, and saint find beauty in danger-ous action and in pursuing an ideal. Kinsella, the exem-plar of the monk, has a stoic control over himself; he emanates a sense of mastery over every situation, in-cluding death. Kinsella views life from the standpoint of duty, with his service for Ireland apparently the high-est duty he can perform. A man of resolute will, Kinsella gave up a career in chemistry to support a brother studying for the priesthood. The brother died before ordination, perhaps sealing Kinsella in his view that the best way to meet the vicissitudes of fortune is with calm-ness and assurance. To a degree he killed the poet in himself, as the poet, Stapleton, asserts. In many in-stances the poet echoes the creed of an aesthete. In his remarks after first sniping at the British soldiers, Stapleton says, " 'The emotion is almost more than I can bear, like listening to music. Yet there is an ele-ment of sensual delight. . . .' " When death closes in on Stapleton after the platoon is forced to withdraw to the General Post Office, he claims that they have reached *"la hora de verdad,* the supreme moment of passion when the whole of life is expressed in a single gesture; when the soul is stripped naked and its real nature is exposed."

As Stapleton indicates, the compact events of Easter Week bring the three figures—soldier, monk, and poet—to a peak of consciousness as they contend with death. Madden somehow feels his own life complete when Kinsella is hit by a bullet; in fact, Madden falls on top of Kinsella. But Madden's last gesture is that of the doomed patriot soldier. Finding no escape, he emerges from a hotel firing two pistols, killing as many of the English as possible.

Perhaps O'Flaherty reached an impasse in designing novels about Ireland after *Insurrection,* for he may have envisioned no further expansion of his theory of evolution in relation to the Irish present or past. In a sense, *Insurrection* serves as a conclusion to his novels on guerrilla warfare and the concomitant themes of consciousness. The struggle of the informer to realize his own individuality, through discovering a sense of guilt, the divided mind of the assassin propelled into violence by a false heroism, and the martyr's futile attempt to hold to an ideal of contemplation as commander of a garrison—these figures reach a culmination in O'Flaherty's embracing view of fulfilled consciousness as the soldier, monk, and poet find an event worthy of complete involvement. For O'Flaherty, Easter Week served as a fitting base for dramatizing the epitome of man's evolution in consciousness.

4

The Irish Psyche after the Revolution

In a half dozen novels O'Flaherty examines the psyche of post-Revolutionary Ireland, a psyche aroused by dreams of national freedom, shocked by the fury of the war against the Black and Tans, and shattered by the atrocities of the Civil War. In these novels O'Flaherty is also dealing with a psyche maimed by the confusion and despair of World War I. As O'Flaherty studies himself and the people of the Irish Free State, he singles out twisted or paralyzed characters, men lost in a fanaticism or obsession they could not recognize. Typically in these novels O'Flaherty isolates an obsession and has it explode in melodramatic action that often destroys the individual. In these six novels the protagonists fall into two groups: in his first two novels the central figures pass through spiritual crises and integrate their personalities, following a pattern close to that of O'Flaherty himself after World War I; in four novels the central figures are damaged or destroyed in the intellectual and spiritual vacuum of the new Ireland. This pattern suggests that after O'Flaherty had written two novels on unifying the powers of his protagonists, he reached out to portray a sense of the void or emptiness pervading modern consciousness. Other novels might be fitted into the second group, for example, his novels on the informer and the assassin, but these works were discussed with the war novels because of their affinities with the Irish Troubles and their emphasis on the violence characteristic of that period. O'Flaherty's gunman and assassin are, in part, belated expressions of dominant images formed during the Troubles.

O'Flaherty's first novel, *Thy Neighbour's Wife,* (1923) was followed almost immediately by *The Black Soul* (1924), as if he wished in the second novel to remove the serious flaws of his first book. Despite significant differences, both novels treat the theme of a young man's struggle with doubt and despair; while the first novel shows a talent for building scene and character, his second novel remains his most coherent artistic work. In *Thy Neighbour's Wife* the protagonist is a young priest, a curate on the largest of the Aran Islands. In *The Black Soul,* O'Flaherty transforms his own life into literary material, centering on a wounded veteran of World War I who regards life as "motion without purpose." But after the war veteran restores his powers, O'Flaherty turns to misfits of the new era, sometimes drifters like Mr. Gilhooley or an aggressive entrepreneur in a provincial Irish town, or misdirected idealists like a modern puritan. O'Flaherty ranges over significant social, economic, and psychological types, writing with passion about the rudderless modern temper. Al-

though O'Flaherty lacks the literary finesse of many recent novelists, he adheres closely to the responsibility of the novelist to present vividly the variety of crises afflicting modern man.

In *Thy Neighbour's Wife* O'Flaherty seems bent on carrying out two purposes which never merge: the conflict of the young curate and a comprehensive view of the folkways on the Aran Islands. He writes expansively and often extravagantly, offering in this novel his most detailed picture of the folkways of the islanders. Somehow he has fallen victim to an epic view of the novel; he feels compelled to present in detail the way of life he had known as a child and youth. But this background does not contribute sufficiently to his anatomy of the passion and skepticism of the young priest. Despite his anticlericalism, O'Flaherty treats with sympathy the interior struggle of the curate who falls in love with the niece of his local parish priest, the curate's religious superior. In addition, the curate doubts for the first time the teachings of the Church, and he discovers the gulf between himself and the common people.

O'Flaherty divides *Thy Neighbour's Wife* into eight parts, eight days in June when the islanders are involved in a number of public gatherings. He dwells at length on Sunday Mass, a Home Rule meeting, the bonfires of St. John's Eve, and a festival of Gaelic games and dances. But O'Flaherty also attempts to dramatize during these eight days a series of crises faced by the young priest—his love for a woman, his struggle with his faith, his jealousy of an island rebel who wins the woman, and the priest's recourse to secret drinking. In this short

time, the priest, Father McMahon, is attacked by forces
that shred his former understanding of himself.

The curate's week begins with the restirring of his
love for the niece of the parish priest. Two years previously, before he was ordained, Father McMahon refused her offer of love. At that time his ambition as
clergyman overrode his affection for the niece, then a
young university graduate. In the interval, Father Mc-
Mahon is ordained and appointed curate on the island.
But when the niece returns as the unhappy wife of a
fifty-five-year-old Irishman who has made a fortune in
South America, the curate reawakens his interest in the
niece but is distressed by his own awkwardness and her
fascination with Hugh O'Malley, an island rebel and a
member of an impoverished aristocratic family. Confused and enraged, the curate drinks secretly. Dead
drunk in his room, he fails to say daily Mass, scandaliz-
ing the housekeeper and the few who attend. He next
agonizes over the dogmas of the Church. By chance he
reads a passage about the early monks on the Aran
Islands. Apparently the monks tested their faith by setting out in an oarless curragh; if they returned, they
were holy; if the boat sank, they were wicked. In a
drunken stupor, Father McMahon resorts to this test,
although he is too drunk to notice the oars in the
curragh that he borrows. A storm arises; the light craft
is tossed about wildly and is about to sink when islandmen rescue him. During the storm the curate undergoes
a radical transformation:

> The curate died. The intellectual died. The visionary
> died. The lover died. The pious, shrinking, conscientious
> priest, fearful of himself, torturing himself with doubts

and temptations, they all died. There remained but Hugh McMahon the man, the human atom, the weak trembling being, with the savage desire to live, to save himself from the yawning chasm of death that was opened up about him by the storm.

Chastened by this ordeal, his soul stripped by a storm that obliterates introspection and reason, the curate counts as nothing his former efforts to write poetry and to be an Irish nationalist. His single concern is now with the Church and his call to be a missionary to China. By placing the conversion in the terror of a storm, O'Flaherty suggests that instinct dominates reason, but he also suggests that the curate becomes a missionary out of fear of death and damnation. In *Thy Neighbour's Wife,* O'Flaherty emphasizes the curate but he admires the spontaneous, independent rebel O'Malley. In his second novel, *The Black Soul,* O'Flaherty gains control over the crisis of his central figure, the use of peasant background, and the development of his theme. In many ways *The Black Soul* is his best novel, but the first novel succeeded eminently in that it won for him the editorial help and friendship of Edward Garnett.

In *The Black Soul* (1924), Fergus O'Connor, the Stranger, like O'Flaherty himself, has lost faith in God, civilization, and himself; he was wounded in World War I, is afflicted with *melancholia acuta,* and has sailed all over the world and worked at odd jobs in Canada. In this novel O'Flaherty allows a full year for the Stranger's recovery and divides the book into four parts, each season corresponding to an inner change in the Stranger.

The Stranger's black soul has been evolving since

childhood. The Stranger recalls that as a child the priest warned the congregation in a small town in the west of Ireland not to send children to his father's school because his father was considered an atheist. The Stranger's black soul accumulated layers of alienation but protected itself with pride, an arrogance that the author calls "his cold aristocratic intellectuality." The questioning self within the Stranger prevented him from enjoying the surface beauty of nature or woman; he could not view either without tormenting himself about the meaning of life and love. Bereft, the Stranger attempted to commit suicide because he had lost faith; to him life was "motion without purpose" and every human act was futile. On Inverara, the island on which he tries to recuperate, the Stranger tries to blot out his black soul through his fondness for Kathleen O'Daly, a schoolteacher and daughter of a publican and magistrate. At first Kathleen embodies for him the peace and innocence that he associated with religion and studies as a young man, but she gradually becomes to him "a shallow conceited woman, just like the artificial unsexed ladies who haunt the suburbs of large cities, full of sham intellectual vanities. . . ."

In *The Black Soul,* however, O'Flaherty concentrates the struggle of the Stranger in the small cabin where he has lodgings. Within the cabin the Stranger contends with the wife and husband, strong individuals who express the creative and destructive forces in the Stranger. The creative force resides in Little Mary, the tallest and most beautiful woman on the island, and the destructive force rests in her husband, Red John, a surly ignorant man who eventually erupts in madness.

Little Mary and Red John have been married five years but communicate mainly in hisses. Because they are childless—Red John has never possessed his wife—he is the butt of jokes, for islandmen regarded the lack of children as a sign of impotence. But Little Mary fits O'Flaherty's view of a wild, beautiful woman; to emphasize this he makes her the natural child of a landlord on the mainland. She regards the peasants as too coarse for her and refuses to associate with the men attracted by her beauty: "Her brain knew nothing of the love of civilization. She knew but the love of nature, that obeys nothing but the blind instinct to fulfill its function and shatter the tool that has achieved its purpose." Little Mary personifies the spontaneity and independence that the Stranger is trying to recover.

Like the priest in *Thy Neighbour's Wife*, the Stranger finds in a storm the means to regain his powers of self. In *The Black Soul* this storm is a battle with another man rather than with the sea. While the Stranger falls into periodic fits of depression and remains in his room, Red John allows weeds to cover his crops, and he pulls out his teeth with pliers and puts them in a cup in the barn. Raging against his wife, Red John strikes his head against a wall. Inevitably the Stranger and Red John fight over Little Mary. During this fight, Red John's scream shocks the Stranger out of a melancholy that has harassed him since the war in France, a shriek that exposes the Stranger's naked self. On a ledge beneath a cliff, with the islanders watching, the Stranger and Red John flail at each other, but Red John's heart breaks and he falls dead. The Stranger flees from the island with Little Mary: "Inverara had rubbed the balm of her fierce strength into his marrows. She had purified his blood with her bitter winds." The Stranger rediscovers a Wordsworthian bond with nature, and Little Mary saves him from the madness and sterility of Red John. Throughout the book brief lyrical passages on the sea, the weather, and the work of the islanders introduce each season, effectively associating the mentality of the Stranger with primal rhythms of nature. These are economic, impressionistic descriptions, a marked contrast to the lengthy sections on folk events and characters of his first novel.

With a confidence in himself and his art acquired through the writing of *The Black Soul*, O'Flaherty turned to the ruins of modern society, to men afflicted with an impaired consciousness. Perhaps the tutoring of Edward Garnett convinced him that art cannot be mixed with propaganda, but in the novels and short stories O'Flaherty does not exploit social injustices in his themes. In the novel written after *The Black Soul*, he began with a lowly form of consciousness in the informer, Gypo Nolan, who becomes aware of himself only through betrayal and guilt. In the novel after *The Informer, Mr. Gilhooley* (1926), he turns to a wasteland of the heart, the sense of emptiness overcoming an engineer as he returns to Ireland after years of work in South America. Mr. Gilhooley becomes a voluptuary; in an earlier generation he could easily have become a companion of Joyce's Simon Dedalus. Because of a slight heart ailment, Gilhooley leaves South America but finds no work in Dublin. With an income of seven hundred pounds a year, he could live anywhere in Ireland, but he drifts from boarding house to boarding

house and spends his time with other men of his years—
Mr. Gilhooley is fifty-two—who have no aspiration
higher than a desire for a regular drink. Gilhooley is
anesthetized to the life around him and takes only a
perfunctory interest in a march of unemployed men.
When drunk, he sometimes dreams of a bee farm. One
of his companions, a poet *manqué,* tells him to live
". . . only where there are green fields and birds and life,
growing and dying and growing and dying, all year
round. Not corruption like this. We're Irish. We were
made for the hillsides and fields. . . ." But Gilhooley's
will is so eroded that he can only dream about a cottage
in the country.

Despite his years, Gilhooley lacks self-knowledge. At
first his life seems to take form when he buys a meal for
a waif, Nelly Fitzpatrick, a twenty-year-old girl who has
been married and fears the return of her husband. But
after she stays a night with Gilhooley, his pity turns to
love, though Nelly is enmeshed in memories of her
young husband and regards Gilhooley only as a kindly,
aging man. What is worse, Gilhooley senses that she does
not love him, but he is so withered emotionally that he
agrees to give Nelly her freedom during the daytime if
she would stay with him at night. Nelly, however, discovers a congenial social life offered by Friel, an estate
agent, a man without intellect but an ingratiating liber-
tine. After learning that Nelly has slept with Friel, Gilhooley strangles Nelly—with no understanding of the
currents of his own jealousy.

In a remarkable set of scenes Gilhooley faces the void;
he peers into an existential abyss. Before he kills Nelly
he has a vision of himself flying over the earth, "a

vapourish grey figure . . . flying with flapping hands into the void." O'Flaherty comments, "The loneliness was so great that it seemed to close in on him, an endless wall of emptiness." After he murders Nelly, Gilhooley rests in a garden for several hours. When he hears the headlines of the murder, he grows defiant, gazes at the water of a canal, muttering, "There is nothing at all, nothing at all." Although the work is often crude and hurried in its presentation, *Mr. Gilhooley* is O'Flaherty's first presentation of modern man's sense of the void.

Just as the malaise of modern Dublin helps to destroy Gilhooley, the drabness of an Irish provincial town contributes to the downfall of its leading men. In *The House of Gold* (1929) O'Flaherty attempts a portrait of an Irish town in the Free State, determined, it seems, to show that this town exchanged one tyranny for another. But in *The House of Gold* the setting is subordinated to the more significant issue of the twisted psyches of several men of the town. Curiously, O'Flaherty boasts in *Shame the Devil* that *The House of Gold* includes a plan for reforming the Irish economy, a plan that in O'Flaherty's view De Valera followed. But O'Flaherty's scheme for cooperatives, for government subsidies for industries and tourist facilities is only a minor part of the novel. Much more remarkable than its economics is the design controlling more diverse material than he had used in any previous model. If O'Flaherty had succeeded in dramatizing fully the parts of his design, *The House of Gold* might indeed provide an Irish equivalent for some of the work of Arnold Bennett or Sinclair Lewis.

In *The House of Gold,* O'Flaherty limits action to a

single day in Barra, a town similar to Galway. He divides the novel into three parts—passion, disintegration, nemesis—a scheme for the movement of the psyches of the leading figures, especially for the protagonist Ramon Mor Costello. Ramon Mor, a peasant, has bought up all the shops and much of the land within twenty miles of Barra. He overpowers everyone in Barra and wins a seat in the Dail or Parliament in Dublin. But the fifty-year-old Ramon Mor's conquests end with his marriage to Nora, a young Dublin girl attracted by Ramon Mor's prestige and strength. Nora comes to a town already corrupted by Ramon Mor's ruthless quest for money, but she brings a beauty unknown to the provincial town, a beauty that incites passions that had not existed before and that cannot be satisfied. O'Flaherty ingeniously blends his study of economic exploitation with the reaction of men to beauty by referring to Nora's golden hair and eyes of a golden shade. Throughout the novel, as he intertwines Ramon Mor's greed and Nora's efforts to satisfy her passions, O'Flaherty periodically points to the cultural vacuum in Irish towns: "For no punishment can be greater for a refined intellect than to be forced to live in an Irish provincial town. Barbarous food, barbarous companionship, an entire lack of social morality, of culture and of intellectual tolerance causes a melancholy that corrupts the strongest mind."

An economic juggernaut, Ramon Mor is an unreflecting man, one who instinctively draws money and property to himself and destroys others standing in his way. Although he worships Nora, he cannot conquer her because of his impotence, a recurring motif in

O'Flaherty's novels. Yet Ramon Mor insists on her sub-
mission. Thwarted in his passion, Ramon Mor suffers a
fatal stroke at the climax of the story, a death fore-
shadowed by a light stroke early in the morning and a
dream in which dogs unsuccessfully pursue a deer.

Ramon Mor's lust for power and money and Nora's
beauty eventually strangle the ambitions of the men
who should be filling out the dream of a new Ireland.
The most independent individual in Barra, ex-rebel
Francis O'Neill, is also an ex-seminarian and an ex-
editor of a Dublin paper. Because of Ramon Mor's
injustices to his father and because Ramon Mor was
profiteering from the men risking their lives for Ireland, O'Neill determines to rob Ramon Mor and flee
with his wife Nora. On the morning of the story,
O'Neill seduces Nora outside of town on a cliff. After
O'Neill and his friends rob Ramon Mor, O'Neill leaves
his companions to pursue Nora. When he finds that she
has committed suicide, he is easily taken by the police.

Another victim of Ramon Mor and Nora is the
doctor, Jim Fitzpatrick. As a young man, Fitzpatrick
became a doctor to help people; inflamed by the nation-
alists' hopes for freedom, he became a revolutionary but
was physically weak and too diffident to follow any ideal
to an end. During the Troubles he was injured; he married his nurse only to find that her slovenly habits
undermined his own enthusiasm for living. At worst a
coward, at best an idealist, Fitzpatrick vacillates between
faith and scepticism, between independence and con-
formity. But Fitzpatrick finally realizes the futility of
his love for Nora and his hatred for Ramon Mor while
he watches a spider play with a reptile. As he overlooks

the town square, noisy with a quarrel between spokesmen for cooperatives and henchmen of Ramon Mor, Fitzpatrick finds a new calm: ". . . it became manifest to him that the desire to appreciate the full sensous and mental pleasure to be derived from a phenomenon, by means of wonder, was probably the main instinct of life." But the doctor's composure is not the tranquility preceding creative thought, for the doctor soon blurs the division between good and evil and passively accepts things as they are, including his slatternly wife and children. Somehow he perceives universal qualities in particular things and regards reality as the completed circle of creation. In Fitzpatrick, O'Flaherty censures an indifference to the physical order and the capacity of some Irishmen to generalize pain and failure into indifference. Yet this large point is not well developed, and O'Flaherty leaves the impression that the doctor will lose himself in empty reverie no matter what the crisis in Barra.

Despite the manifold perspectives in *The House of Gold,* they do not converge into a telling unity, and many parts of his theme of passion, disintegration, and nemesis are dissipated in melodramatic fragments.

After the abortive diatribe against war in *The Return of the Brute* in 1929, O'Flaherty turned to the puritan mentality that ran rampant in the first years of the Free State. Yeats scorns this outlook in his speeches on censorship and divorce; O'Flaherty rails against the puritans in *A Tourist's Guide to Ireland* (1930), a reaction generated in part by the appearance of his novels on the list of censored books. Despite intrinsic difficulties as a work of art, *The Puritan* (1931) stands as one of the most penetrating studies of the modern Irish puritan. In the novel O'Flaherty successfully isolates a rhythm of experience that drives an individual to interfere with the conduct of others. This novel fits the traditional pattern of puritan consciousness in which the attack that an aggressive individual makes against the sins of others blinds him to his own faults.

O'Flaherty's protagonist, a twenty-four-year-old Dublin journalist, ultimately recognizes the evil in a murder that he once thought a purifying act. But in one respect the unfolding actions gradually distract the reader more and more, for he learns that the journalist, Francis Ferriter, kills a whore in the rooming house where he stays, that Ferriter has written a manifesto called "The Sacrifice of Blood," and that the police inspector gives Ferriter freedom so that he will incriminate himself. Given these events and attitudes, the reader cannot avoid unfavorable comparisons between *The Puritan* and Dostoevsky's *Crime and Punishment*. But O'Flaherty's intention is severely limited in comparison to Dostoevsky's, for he examines only a single figure in detail; he does not build up a large number of secondary figures that enlarge the theme; nor does O'Flaherty pursue the combined themes of suffering and redemption. Instead, O'Flaherty emphasizes the puritan's act of murder and the intense introspection that it precipitates.

As in his other novels, O'Flaherty uses melodrama to compel his protagonists to recognize their moral blindness. In this novel the puritan receives repeated shocks to his ego before he perceives evil in murdering the whore. Ferriter commits the murder at the opening of the novel, and O'Flaherty follows the steps that Ferriter takes after the murder. Immediately after killing the whore, Teresa Burke, Ferriter blames Dr. O'Leary, a frequent visitor who has loved Teresa for some years but because of parental interference has been unable to marry her. Ferriter importunes his editor to print a story in which O'Leary is accused of the murder, but the editor is too astute for Ferriter and fires him. When Ferriter later tries to compel the police to arrest O'Leary, a wise inspector, like Porfiry Petrovitch in *Crime and Punishment,* allows Ferriter twenty-four hours of freedom. In distress, Ferriter feels that he may expiate his crime only by losing his own innocence. Under the eyes of a detective, Ferriter walks through the red-light district and has bizarre conversations with one and then with three whores. At midnight Ferriter returns to the police inspector, who acknowledges that Ferriter, now on the edge of madness, has paid a severe penalty for his crime.

As a novel, *The Puritan* rushes along, its energies channeled into a rapid exposé of Ferriter's discovery of evil in himself. Unwittingly Ferriter developed the puritan side of his personality. On the death of his father, Ferriter has to give up the study of law to earn his living as a journalist. But he fails as a journalist and soon becomes a bigot and a man who blames his failure on others. He joins a militant society to suppress vice, seeing himself as a crusader, a lonely hero in his decision to stamp out vice by killing a whore: "Had he not seen himself as the leader of this holy war while the divine fire of fanaticism was preparing him to commit the murder? Was not the manuscript in his wallet a treatise on the divine right to conduct such a war?" Ferriter resigns from the society because of the hypocrisy of its leaders who would never accuse anyone in power. Like O'Flaherty's assassin, the puritan takes upon himself the responsibility for reforming society. As he confesses to a priest, Ferriter, rambling on about his past, includes this explanation of the murder: " 'You must know what I have done was purely an experiment on my part, in order to prove to myself and to all humanity whether God exists or not. I also wished to prove, in the second place but of equal importance with the first, whether man has a divine destiny.' " But after the murder he seeks to identify two parts of himself that are combating each other. Ferriter's knowledge of self expands under the pressure to account for his own brutality: " 'I have come to the conclusion that each human soul is the nest of a multitude of personalities each of which represents a cycle of experience and that the body is the field of battle on which they struggle for mastery.' " Why had the personality of the murderer crowded out other potentialities? As Ferriter visits his mother and relatives, he gradually sees his own fanaticism. He recalls that he was attracted to Teresa Burke, the whore, by a photograph of her as an innocent schoolgirl. In memory Ferriter relives his visit to her apartment, her effort to seduce him, her later willingness to attend church with him, evidence to him of her repentance. Finally, he asks himself, "Did I really love her? Did I do it through jealousy?" In confessing to the priest, he says that he rehearsed everything to the very sensation of plunging a knife into her back, but he did not think at all of what would come afterward. Like Gilhooley, Ferriter faces the emptiness of the cold interstellar spaces. Instead of becoming a hero as he expected, Ferriter sinks into the despair of a man remorsefully aware of the destructive forces within. Unlike Raskolnikov, he finds no Sonja to initiate his restoration, or in O'Flaherty's terms, Ferriter has no means of exorcising his black soul. The novel remains a rough-hewn though compelling portrait of the puritan mentality in modern Ireland.

Another novel might be added to O'Flaherty's studies of disillusionment in the Irish Free State, *Hollywood Cemetery* (1935). The book was written and published immediately after the filming of *The Informer*. In this novel O'Flaherty satirizes the commercialized imagination of Hollywood, but his plodding realistic scenes often seem like a caricature of Hollywood folklore. O'Flaherty's cumbersome episodes lack satiric bite, although his imagination catches fire in the final scene of the book.

The Irish characters in *Hollywood Cemetery,* a writer and a country girl who is transformed by Hollywood agents into an actress, succumb to the mania for money and publicity. The Irish writer, a proletarian novelist, Brian Carey, writes a book about an Irish girl who migrates to America; after a reckless life in the new country, she and her lover die in an electric chair. Carey's Irish-American novel attracts a director bent on using the work in his campaign to improve the quality of films. A producer and director search Ireland for a leading woman to shoot scenes of the countryside. The stage designer, however, insists that he can create a more authentic Irish village in Hollywood than is available in Ireland. The producer finds his star in a barmaid; he renames her Angela Devlin to describe the angelic and diabolical qualities that he thinks she combines. Later, before the film party returns to America, the producer decides to turn Angela Devlin into a Veiled Goddess, a symbol of romantic love that would purify the film industry and lift America out of the depression.

Carey and Angela Devlin revolt against the vulgarity and outlandish publicity stunts of the producer Mortimer. As a producer Mortimer bullies his colleagues but is thwarted only when he tries to seduce Angela Devlin. Once in America, Mortimer imprisons Angela Devlin in his fortified house to train her as the Veiled Goddess. Meanwhile, Mortimer sends out press releases about her beauty that will revive ideal love as soon as Americans see her on the screen. But an Irish-American society that punishes anyone tarnishing the good name of Ireland kidnaps Angela Devlin and Brian Carey, and flies them to Mexico, where the plane crashes. The pilot is killed, and Angela and Carey, free from the lunacy of Hollywood, marry in a Mexican village.

In this novel, O'Flaherty's invention soars only in the final scene. His satire takes form in a fantasy, a scene equaled in his work in the privately printed story, "The Ecstasy of Angus" (1931). Fearful that Angela might not cooperate as the Veiled Goddess, Mortimer trains a substitute for her, an effeminate actor who mimics every mannerism of Angela; his mimicking is so accurate that Angela Devlin is terrified when she sees her double. Mortimer's caution in preparing a double, however, saves his reputation even though he deceives the public. Once the cry arises that she does not exist, he is compelled to display the Veiled Goddess.

In this final scene O'Flaherty penetrates further than ever before into the godless world of the twentieth century; at the same time he mocks the commercial spirit in art that readily creates debased idols. When the cars carrying the Veiled Goddess and her entourage enter Hollywood Boulevard, a group of kneeling women dressed in white hold a banner saying, "The league of screen mothers dedicate their children to the pure and romantic love personified by Angela Devlin." On the other side of the street are two groups of men wearing flour sacks with another banner, "Welcome to the Cemetery of the Living Dead." When the people look upon the substitute Veiled Goddess, their faces become distorted by a passion that the narrator says is neither good nor evil, but something primitive, something long forgotten by civilization. Mortimer calls the appearance of the Veiled Goddess the greatest moment in history. Some people go into fits and roll about; others froth at the mouth; others become lewd; some tear their hair and garments. There is a cry, " 'She is. She is. She is.' " The crowd takes up the cry, repeating it with renewed frenzy. The egregious plan of Mortimer releases a dionysiac madness. Has the male Veiled Goddess broken the barrier of good and evil and reached the ecstasy described by Nietzsche? Or are these people deluded by the degraded art of Hollywood, their emotions set on a dizzying course that they cannot recognize? The general sweep of the novel supports this latter reading. More ominous is the phrase that Hollywood is a cemetery for the living dead, a phrase used earlier in the book in a Communist paper's analysis of the movies. Mortimer's perverse ingenuity in creating a false Veiled Goddess seems to have generated on one side an uncontrolled wildness and on the other a despairing passivity, withering evidence of the damage done the psyche by the image-makers of Hollywood.

5

The Short Stories

The short stories of Liam O'Flaherty have not received the attention that they merit, even though he is generally mentioned in the company of such masters as Frank O'Connor and Sean O'Faolain. Indeed, almost every critic, including William Troy in his seminal articles on O'Flaherty (*Bookman,* 1929), begins with the point that O'Flaherty is a writer who has been neglected too long. O'Flaherty himself placed less emphasis on his short stories than on his novels, but in his first decade as a writer he published three collections of short stories: *Spring Sowing* (1924), *The Tent* (1926), and *The Mountain Tavern* (1929). A selection from these volumes was published in 1937 and has been reprinted occasionally. Several new stories make up *Two Lovely Beasts* (1948), and during and after World War II he wrote stories in Irish that were published in *Duil* (1953). By contrast, his contemporaries, O'Faolain and O'Connor, did not publish collections of short stories until the 1930s: O'Connor's *Guests of the Nation* appearing in 1931, and O'Faolain's *Midsummer Night's*

Madness in 1932. But O'Connor and O'Faolain wrote their first books about the Revolution. As young men they had participated in it and shared its ideals and disillusionment, and they spoke more directly than did O'Flaherty to the new Ireland and its problems. In addition, O'Connor and O'Faolain were intimately connected with the theater, magazines, and literary movements, whereas O'Flaherty withdrew from the literary scene and literary politics in about 1927. What attention O'Flaherty aroused came through his novels rather than his short stories.

Yet O'Flaherty's short stories will continue to attract readers to themselves and to his novels like *The Black Soul* and *Skerrett*. For in the short stories, despite the apparent speed with which they were written, O'Flaherty builds in deceptively simple stories vivid images of the basic instincts of man. Somehow by stripping away the covering of civilization and the superstructures of reason, he penetrated to a bedrock of experience. It is indeed a complex critical problem to account for the simplicity and directness of his best short stories. To O'Flaherty these stories were secondary to the larger themes and characters of his novels; in fact, the stories sometimes resemble vignettes that could be extracted from his novels on the Aran Islands and the west of Ireland.

O'Flaherty's choice of peasants and animals as subject matter for his stories remains something of a mystery, despite Edward Garnett's instruction that he return to Ireland and write about cows, eels, and country matters instead of sensational stories about London. O'Flaherty's first stories, rejected by editors, were written in response to his reading de Maupassant while working in Connecticut. The Frenchman's bold exposure of peasant life may have stimulated O'Flaherty to write about peasants in a manner different from that of Yeats, A.E., and Synge. Besides, O'Flaherty's traumatic experience in the war and his years of wandering as seaman and miscellaneous worker may have sent him back, in imagination, to the certainties of his childhood on Inishmore. One suspects too that O'Flaherty's sympathy with Communistic causes helped him to discern a stability and permanence in peasant life in contrast to the flux and degradation of the proletariat. Through contemplating simple people and animals and the relatively uncomplicated forces of nature O'Flaherty may have hoped to present an instinctive response to a life that had been mangled or smothered by industrialization, cities, and wars.

This search for an accurate rendering of man's instinctive life marks both his short stories and his novels. In the novels, oversized Dostoevskian figures dominate the work; their dreams of perfection, twisted and fanatic as they generally are, represent man's upward movement to a perfection implicit in the evolutionary process. In the short stories O'Flaherty falls back on peasants, animals, and children; the setting is that of farm, sea, or village. As early as 1929, William Troy speculated on the Gaelic qualities in O'Flaherty's work: "He is closer to the unknown writers of the early Gaelic folk literature than to any of his contemporaries. He is less the product of any modern school than of that period when European culture had not yet entirely lost its innocence." In both novels and short stories, a Gaelic influence is manifest in the directness of narrative, the simplicity of language, and an elemental concern with primary emotions. One of the most noticeable differences between novels and short stories, however, lies in the use of melodrama, which is employed in the novels mainly in the interest of psychological realism. Melodrama seems to be his technique for showing the explosive emotions of his protagonists; for O'Flaherty it is a means to express a heightened level of intensity. The short stories, however, seem to be born in a different literary climate. Sean O'Faolain noted this difference in 1937 when a collected edition of O'Flaherty's stories was published. He questions the melodrama in the novels but praises the composure of the short stories. Among novelists, he says, O'Flaherty is a Don Quixote, an inverted romantic in search for an ideal beauty, hard to define because of the fury with which he rushes against his enemies. But the short stories have a different ambience: "In those lovely short stories, however, he is at rest. There he has found something that bears resemblance to his ideal, not in men, but in birds and animals; and often men are seen as cruel creatures who hunt and torment these dumb things."

Although O'Flaherty's stories deal mainly with peasants and animals, he wrote a small number of stories about war. In these stories his sympathies lie with the common soldier and the common people. In a brief sketch called "The Sniper," he withholds until the end the fact that brother has killed brother during Ireland's Civil War of 1922–23. He concentrates on the pain of a bullet wound rather than on the circumstances or causes of the Civil War; his concern is with the concrete inci-

dent and emotions of the soldiers. In this story the open,
matter-of-fact presentation of the shooting and the pain
of the wound makes the revelation that brother has shot
brother the final atrocity in a barbaric world. In "The
Mountain Tavern," another story of the Irish Civil
War, two Republican soldiers carry a wounded comrade
through a snowstorm, hoping to find refuge in a mountain tavern. When they reach their goal, they find the
tavern a smoking ruins. The strength of the story lies in
the multiple sympathies of the narrator. After attending
to the wounded soldier whose red blood colors the snow,
he shifts attention to the woman who owns the tavern.
This woman says that the soldier did not die for her, and
she repeats the word *robbers,* like a refrain, to describe
both Republicans and Free-Staters. For her, three years
of fighting have destroyed her home and livelihood. A
few civilians standing by regard the soldiers "with the
serene cruelty of children watching an insect being
tortured." In another story called simply, "Civil War,"
in which the Republicans are defeated in a four-day
skirmish, a cowardly man destroys a brave soldier as
well as himself. To O'Flaherty, who has Nietzschean
proclivities, the act of the weak destroying the strong is
a heinous offense against mankind.

O'Flaherty's prevailing concern, however, is not with
war but with peasants and animals, or as one critic
states, with the land. His purpose is not to present a
realistic or naturalistic view of the Irish peasant; his
stories lack the harsh objectivity and ironies of Chek-
hov's story "Peasants," a severe indictment of the ignorance, drunkenness and brutality of the peasant, and
a more severe indictment of the masters permitting this

suffering. Instead, O'Flaherty generally uses the simplicity of peasant life to depict elemental reactions and instincts. Although he does not ignore cruelty, ignorance, or the sporadic eruptions of rage or madness among the peasants, he uses character and event to dramatize the uncluttered working out of creative and destructive forces in man and nature. He prizes feats of strength, unexpected moments of joy and grief, those dramatic interstices in man's struggle against social and natural forces that may injure or annihilate him.

Critics have difficulty in assigning causes to the world view in O'Flaherty's short stories. The achievement still outruns theories, but somehow in these stories O'Flaherty recaptures a state of mind of one who has just conquered his black soul. It will be recalled that the Stranger in *The Black Soul* suffers from a mordant introspection; he cannot enjoy nature or people without losing himself in analysis and self-doubt; having lost faith in God, civilization, and himself, he sinks into despair. By freeing himself from the necessity of making an intellectual gloss on objects and people, O'Flaherty concentrates on people, things, and events with his full energies devoted to expressing their intrinsic being. He takes peasantlike delight in an unfettered examination of a wave, the birth of a cow, a daughter going into exile; the object, person, or event so captivates his imagination that nothing seems to intrude between the author and the unfolding of the destiny of his subject. In this state of mind he writes with a clear-eyed intensity and immediacy that seems almost a total surrender of the author's personality to the nature of things outside of himself.

Collectively O'Flaherty's short stories describe two or three generations of life in the Aran Islands and the west of Ireland; perhaps they reach back even further, so little did life change in those areas until the end of the nineteenth century. In the short stories, O'Flaherty makes little effort to assign a time to the events; peasants have always fished from the cliffs, fought the sea, and tilled their fields. In a story like "The Reaping Race," the prize of five pounds for skill in cutting grain is offered by an engineer, an offer that may not have been made until the end of the century, but the story deals with differences in character among three strong men with pride flowing from a lifetime spent in the fields. Bodkin hurries and tires; in the afternoon he develops a thirst and cannot stop drinking cold tea, thus eliminating himself from the race. Considine holds to the old custom of eating while working, but he collapses at about four o'clock in the afternoon, and Gill takes twenty minutes off for lunch, works deliberately, and as the only man to finish, wins the five-pound note. O'Flaherty's fable pits simple men against each other and nature.

Among peasants O'Flaherty has a fondness for crotchety and slovenly old people, eccentric individuals who see themselves as bearers of a tradition. Perhaps his most impressive creation of this type is Brian Kilmartin in *Famine,* a man who clings to his land despite the famine, knowing that bad years will be followed by good years. Often these peasants are upset by new leaders, new money, and new goods. For instance, Stoney Batter, a bachelor, has his house chosen as the site of the "confessions" that occur every twelve years in the village; for the confessions the priest visits one of the twenty-four houses for the sacraments and Mass. Stoney's house is so dirty and cluttered that the villagers fear the sting of disgrace. To resolve the problem, Stoney is forced to deed the house to his brother, a married man, the most respectable man in the village. The house is cleaned, and the confessions proceed with honor to the village. But after eight months, Louisa Derrane, the woman who cleaned the cottage, returns, claiming to be pregnant by Stoney. In turn Stoney claims that she stayed with his brother, Peter, at night. Enraged, Peter attacks Stoney with a spade. The parish priest has Peter pay for the bastard, and Peter's wife returns to him. On Peter's order the police evict Stoney from the cottage, and he dies in a workhouse. But in the conclusion O'Flaherty suddenly alters our view of Stoney Batter as a victim of the community's desire for respectability, for the narrator recalls that as a boy he admired the independence of Stoney Batter as a man who did not work. In addition the narrator as a boy bought piglets that publicans took from Stoney for his drinking debts.

One of O'Flaherty's flamboyant spokesmen for the traditional ways is a testy eighty-year-old man, an ex-pilot named Tom. In "Galway Bay," Tom quarrels with everyone on the steamer as he brings his cattle to the city. The old man had wrested his cattle from his daughter and son-in-law, for although he had given them his farm, he saved the cattle for himself. As he surveys the vista of islands, mainland, the Cliffs of Moher, and the mountains of Connemara, he asserts: " 'All this belongs to us,' cried the old man arrogantly, 'to us, true men of the west. We are a breed by ourselves. We are people of the islands and of all the land that does border on the western sea. We want no foreigners to come interfering with us, putting laws around our necks, like you put a spancel on a wicked goat. We have the spunk in us and we'll take the sway from all comers. We are a breed on our own.' " The old man's speech is directed at "foreigners," tourists on board the steamer.

O'Flaherty is sensitive to the discipline of the peasant code, for it demands courage, reticence, and a self-abnegation that is sometimes terrifying in its implications. In family life there is little room for emotional display. In "Going into Exile," a father longs to embrace his son before the son and daughter leave for America, but he does not do so. And the mother, near hysteria, utters only a few commonplaces to her daughter. Yet, for another kind of suffering, the loss of a daughter's virtue, there may be an open expression of grief. In "The Letter," O'Flaherty concludes with the pathos of a family lament in the field; the father has just read a letter from his daughter in America. She has sent twenty pounds and a brief note on how much she hates her life in America because of what the country has done to her.

Among peasants, class lines may also restrict emotional fulfillment. In "The Touch," a father prevents his daughter from looking at a day-laborer; the father believes that a man without a penny should not speak to his daughter. In the daughter's mind, the day-laborer's covert touch is all the love that she will ever know, so narrow are the channels of life in this world. In O'Flaherty's stories there are few love scenes, and those few are not well developed, but he senses the unstated affection that unifies a family or holds individuals together in a world in which untimely death is frequent. Like Synge, O'Flaherty finds some of his most poignant stories in separation and loss. "The Stream" is an uncomplicated presentation of a young woman's loss of her husband. The new husband follows the call of his friends to hunt birds' eggs on a cliff, where he has a fatal accident. The young widow curses all things young; then "her body withered until it was like her soul."

O'Flaherty does not escape some of the pitfalls of stories about peasants. Some yarns, possibly adapted from the oral tradition, seem to have only a surface; the author delights in too facile an exaggeration or in a comic hoax. In "The Pot of Gold," for example, Rogers convinces three friends that they should look in nearby hills for gold that he saw one night in a dream. In his dream there was a flat rock with red moss in a corner; under a rock there was a dead black cat, and under the cat, gold. The four men steal into the hills at night and locate the rock and the black cat. While the others are digging up the cat, Rogers runs home. The three men recognize the cat as one from the village, but they are afraid to have Rogers arrested for killing a cat: they would expose their own foolishness. O'Flaherty seems to enjoy the clever anecdote in such stories as "The Stolen Ass" and "A Shilling." One of his best stories with pathos and humor is "A Red Petticoat." A widow who tells stories and sings songs to still the hunger pangs of her children finds that her art can no longer substitute for an empty larder. Known as Mary of the Bad Verses because of the bite of her curse, the widow goes to a shop and accuses the shopkeeper, Mrs. Murtagh, of wearing a red petticoat on a nocturnal visit to the tailor. In the vixenish quarrel that follows, the shopkeeper denies that she wore a red petticoat; she was wearing a black skirt. The fight continues, and just as customers enter, the widow feigns an attack and slumps to the floor. In the presence of the customers, the widow claims that the shopkeeper gladly extends credit to her. And the embarrassed shopkeeper gives her a large supply of groceries, then hustles her out of the shop.

Some of O'Flaherty's yarns are lively expressions of the gaucherie of country people and have the flavor of Lady Gregory's *Spreading the News*. At times O'Flaherty depends on unwarranted surprise and an emphasis on local color. If seldom these stories, unlike his best works, are undergirded by a persisting rhythm of life, they can be said to reveal his understanding of folktales and yarns. In "The Beggars," a blind beggar has a dream that he will collect a great deal of money at a racetrack, although he has never visited such a place. At the track, he is enraged because he is the only beggar who does not receive any coins. But a singing woman gives him a sandwich and saves him from a riderless horse, and a drunken man gives him a five-pound note. The tale reflects O'Flaherty's interest in racing and testifies to the generosity of beggars, but it hardly penetrates beneath the surface of its material.

Generally, however, O'Flaherty's stories about peasants form a simple, rather severe world in which poverty and nature compete with men for mastery, in which the daily or seasonal round of work exhibits basic instincts of men. While he may be considered a long-term optimist, O'Flaherty is sadly aware that each living thing completes its part in the evolutionary process through its own destruction. In method, O'Flaherty's stories have a simplicity that suggests Hemingway's studied effort to select specific details that create scene or character and provide at the same time the means to elicit the right emotional reaction. But O'Flaherty selects his details on a much simpler level. He is not interested in symbolism as such; he relies on an inherent rather than on an analogical symbolism. He uses the natural order as a Gaelic storyteller, because of his interest in the person or event itself; he depends on the narrative movement of the story. One critic, Michael Murray, notes that O'Flaherty is most effective when he remains close to the oral tradition, when the storyteller presents events and people simply and directly. When O'Flaherty indulges in philosophy or manipulates symbolism or overstates themes, his stories tend to collapse. But as indicated above, the oral tradition may also beguile O'Flaherty through ingenious situations. O'Flaherty's achievement in the short story may best be grasped, I believe, by considering two types of stories in which he excelled: the lyric sketch and the comprehensive fable. Both types, as used by O'Flaherty, have close ties with the oral tradition and O'Flaherty's search to discover or rediscover an elemental life in man.

By far the greatest number of O'Flaherty's stories are lyric sketches, with a simple narrative, a limited plot, and with scene and characterization governed by what is immediate and readily observable. O'Flaherty does not neglect the narrative, but the effect of the narrative in his shortest works is similar to that of a lyric poem;

in fact, as John Zneimer observes, in these sketches the entire story is an epiphany. The uncomplicated plot discloses the inevitable working out of an emotion or a rhythm of nature. There is little attention to any causal arrangement of events; O'Flaherty holds tightly to the present tense; people speak and act; storms arise and fall without analysis. In the short stories, as in the novels, he does not experiment with point of view; he utilizes a reliable narrator who is clear-eyed, sane, and shrewdly alert to the forces in man, society, and nature, that maim or crush the individual. Neither does he psychoanalyze his characters; he has little use for flashbacks or the probings of memory. Similarly, O'Flaherty limits his language to ordinary words; at times he lapses into pedestrian phrases or clichés; he disdains style. In his theory the raw urgency of action and reaction should not be impeded by fastidious diction. Yet in the best of his lyric sketches, O'Flaherty places his men and women close to the earth or sea in narrative that is stark, unsophisticated, and accurate for evoking a sense of the relentless working out of man's instincts.

O'Flaherty's stories lack the breadth and complexity of those of Joyce, O'Faolain, or O'Connor, and he deals with an external world foreign to men in an industrial, urban society. Yet his simple world is perfectly attuned to the passions and instincts that he wishes to stress. Like Yeats and Lawrence, he selects his material to rediscover the wellsprings of man's emotional life. Although he does not explore as widely as these writers, he acquires, as Yeats would say, an intensity through simplification. His setting, characters, and language cling to the physical order in which all men must live, despite their attachment to cities and the demands of reason. Frequently O'Flaherty writes of man's bond with the earth as a source of life and wisdom. In "Spring Sowing," for example, he describes a young couple's first day of work in the fields. They are slightly chilled by the frost and by the uncertainty of their relationship to each other. As Martin takes his spade, he tells Mary that she will see what kind of a man she has, but Mary replies that she will wait until sunset to judge. As Martin turns the first sod, Mary drops the seeds on a ridge, runs up and puts her arms around his waist; he tells her to stay back: "Suppose anybody saw us trapesing about like this in the field of our spring sowing." O'Flaherty dwells briefly on the double-edged thought of Mary as she continues to gaze at the field that will mark out her life: "She became suddenly afraid of that pitiless, cruel earth, the peasant's slave master, that would keep her chained to hard work and poverty all her life until she would sink again into its bosom." For a moment she feels that her new love has vanished. But Martin works furiously to complete the day's planting: "They had done it together. They had planted seeds in the earth. The next day and the next and all their lives, when spring came they would have to bend their backs and do it until their hands and bones got twisted with rheumatism. But night would always bring sleep and forgetfulness." The course of their lives, their ultimate fate, is expressed in miniature in their first day of work together.

O'Flaherty sometimes uses the lyric sketch to dramatize a peasant's encounter with death, generally with an appreciation for the awesome beauty to be found in incidents of mortal danger. In "Trapped," a young man gathering birds' eggs on a cliff is stranded because of crumbling rock; his path to the top of a cliff is cut off. Rigid with fear, he descends a steep-edged rock that no one had been on before. As he starts to swim in water infested with sharks, he regains his pride, praying and thinking of what the villagers will say of his feat. For the fishermen of Aran, death was imminent in the sudden storms at sea, whose importance in their lives is described by a woman in "Landing": " 'Sure we only live by the Grace of God, sure enough. With the sea always watching to devour us. And yet only for it we would starve.' " The convergence of life and death in the sea also dominates "The Oar." Two curraghs, with three men each, are fishing by moonlight. A school of bream sweeps by them, and so intent are the fishermen on filling their boats that they ignore a storm. When it breaks they row feverishly but they become engrossed with their skill as well as with their fear: "Now the men did not pull fiercely but cautiously. They measured out half and quarter strokes, saving their boats from the foam-capped monstrous waves that jumped at them from out the lightning flashes." But then Red Bartly, the leader of one boat, sees water like a falling cliff filling the other boat; through lightning flashes he and his men see an upraised oar, held by a man in great pain. Refusing to risk pursuit of the other curragh, Red Bartly explains, "Three widows are enough." Despite their skill and courage, one crew is destroyed, the other saved. Red Bartly and his men cannot forget the upraised oar: "It followed us and no hand was grasping it."

In O'Flaherty's lyric sketches, children often reveal parts of man's instinctive life. Through children he adds to the simplicity of peasants the quality of innocence, an un-self-conscious immersion in desires and fears. In "The Wren's Nest," for instance, the unthinking cruelty of boys is as remorseless as that of men in trenches. In this story, two boys dare each other to climb a cliff. As they climb they see a wren with her little ones. In fighting over possession of the nest, the boys knock it down; the wrens fly away, and a small egg falls to the ground without breaking. Later the boys walk by the wrens without noticing the birds; but if they had, the author comments, they would have thrown stones. For O'Flaherty, the youngsters also retain a sense of awe and wonder at the great commonplaces of life, like the birth of animals. In "Three Lambs," a country boy eagerly runs through the morning grass to be present at a lambing. When he sees three lambs born from one sheep, he shares the simple joy of the girl in Browning's "Pippa Passes."

In the lyric sketches, O'Flaherty sometimes brings his exploration of man's instincts to a sharp focus by using animals, which permits him to strip away the distorting colors of civilization. In his best stories of animals he is seldom pedantic or moralistic, although he occasionally adds a philosophical statement to press home a theme. In stories like "The Conger Eel," he concentrates on a single eel, its wildness and strength, its insatiable appetite, and its desire for freedom of movement. The eel is eight feet long, two feet in circumference, a black mysterious body that frightens a school of mackerel: "The thousand blue and white bodies flashed and shimmered in the sun for three moments, and then they disappeared, leaving a large patch of the dark water convulsing turbulently." After scattering the mackerel, the eel swims into a fishing net and is terrified by the black strands standing upright in the water; he is caught in a maze of fish: "Then the eel began to struggle fiercely to escape. He hurtled hither and thither, swinging his long slippery body backwards and forwards, ripping with his snout, surging forward suddenly at full speed churning the water. He ripped and tore the net, cutting great long gashes in it. But the more he cut and ripped the more deeply enmeshed did he become." He releases the mackerel, but not himself. When he is hauled into a curragh, an old fisherman curses him and a young man is terrified. When the young man cuts the net, the eel falls to the bottom of the boat, rocking the frail craft as he beats the sides with his tail. " 'Strike him on the nable,' " the old man cries repeatedly. The fishermen are cursing and panting as they strike at the eel. Finally the young man lifts the eel in his arms and drops him into the water, where he immediately swims to the bottom: "Then stretching out to his full length he coursed in a wide arc to his enormous lair, far away in the silent depths." In the story the eel becomes something of a demonic force, scattering the mackerel, endangering the fishermen, and rousing all his strength to find his home in obscure depths beyond the reach of man.

The lyric sketches of animals are not always related to the demonic or the destructive aspect of nature. Any of the primary emotions may be emphasized. For instance, in "The Cow's Death," O'Flaherty renders through his account of a cow and a stillborn calf the pathos of mother love. The author depicts every move of the cow as it follows the path on which the stillborn calf was dragged and thrown over a cliff into the sea. The cow forces its way through fences; she crosses small stony fields and frets in bewilderment at the edge of the cliff: "She stopped again, seeing nothing about her in the field. Then she began to run around by the fence, putting her head over it here and there, lowing. She found nothing. Nothing answered her call. She became wilder as the sense of her loss became clearer to her consciousness." As the cow can pick up no scent of the calf, she follows an imperious instinct: "And the cow, uttering a loud bellow, jumped headlong down."

In such works as this, O'Flaherty exposes instincts outside of Victorian pieties or the longings of the Celtic Twilight. Yet he does not adhere to the naturalistic practice of using animals to show that man is trapped by his surroundings; he is not a strict determinist. Because his milieu is the field and sea rather than the slum, the factory, or the mine, he readily allows for acts arising from the strength, courage, or desperation of man or animal. In addition, O'Flaherty, as we have seen, is committed to an evolutionary view in which every being has a core of energy, an entelechy, that must be fulfilled even if that fulfillment brings about injury or death. In "The Hawk," for instance, a hawk attacks a lark and stuns it. On the second rush the hawk kills the lark instantly and takes the carcass to his mate on the edge of a cliff, after carefully luring away other birds from the ledge. At this point, O'Flaherty interprets, "His brute soul was exalted by the consciousness that he had achieved the fullness of the purpose for which nature had endowed him." This rather ponderous sentence intrudes upon the narrative, but O'Flaherty seems de-

termined to stress the brute soul in man by the compli-
cations that he adds to the story. Three men climb near
the ledge; the hawk attacks the eyes of one of the men
who beats off the bird and captures the female, putting
the female and her egg into his sack. Thus the instinctive rapacity of the hawk is complemented by the casual
wantonness of man. The narrator does not comment on
the action of the man, but with the addition of men to
the story he suggests that animal and man are closely
related in the process of destroying life.

When animals are at the center of the lyric sketches,
O'Flaherty shows us his openness to the wild, uninhib-
ited forces of nature; he taps a pristine depth and purity
in nature familiar now to many readers from transla-
tions from the Gaelic. In "The Wounded Cormorant," a
falling rock is loosened by a goat; it rolls down to a rock
in the sea on which a flock of cormorants is sitting. One
of the birds is struck on the leg; he utters a scream, and
the other birds watch as his leg dangles crookedly. The
flock of birds flies out to sea to discover their enemy:
"But the wounded one rushed about in the water flapping its wings in agony. The salt brine stung the wound,
and it could not stand still. After a few moments it rose
from the sea and set off at a terrific rate, flying along the
face of the cliff, mad with pain." Other cormorants peck
at the wounded leg, and when the flock goes out to sea
to gather momentum to land on a higher ledge, the
wounded cormorant makes a smaller circle and forces
itself to try a landing on the new level. O'Flaherty re-
minds the reader of an implacable law: "At all costs it
must reach them or perish. Cast out from the flock,
death was certain." But when the wounded bird lands,

the other cormorants try to push it back; one bird prods its right eye, another grips the wounded leg in its beak, tearing the leg. Finally the wounded cormorant is pushed off the ledge, flutters its wings, and sinks into the sea. The agony of the bird and its merciless exclusion from the flock evokes the sense of all ostracism and exile.

O'Flaherty's lyric sketches sometimes expand to embrace a cycle of experience with distinct parts, a shift that makes these stories close to conventionally plotted stories. In the few stories in this group, he often crowds the story toward allegory, but affinities with the lyric sketch remain strong. For instance, in "The Black Rabbit," he embodies part of his thesis on the evolutionary nature of life processes. In this view, the intellect of man moves toward perfection. Men's concepts and images of the deity reflect their grasp of this ultimate perfection; and such positions as skepticism, cynicism, and agnosticism are self-defeating because they restrict a vigorous pursuit of perfection. These insights lead O'Flaherty to censure individuals and tendencies in society that block a gifted man's quest for perfection. In "The Black Rabbit," the rabbit grows large and aggressive, "a sport of nature, a sudden upward curve in the direction of perfection and divine intellect; indeed, he was like that first monkey that became inspired with the vision of humanity." Yet the black rabbit inspires a hatred and fear among ignorant people as he grows more daring and complex. He frightens a housekeeper who determines to destroy him. First she has a fierce cat come into the back garden; later a group of wild cats manage to destroy the black rabbit. As in his earlier story, "The

Civil War," O'Flaherty demonstrates the capacity of the
timid and mediocre to halt the upward movement of
man. But in this story the thesis has carried the narrative
too far from the inevitable, natural events that mark
his best stories.

In O'Flaherty's comprehensive fables or parables, a
series of simple episodes acquire coherence and vitality
from rather extensive substructures. Surprisingly, in
view of the simplicity and directness of the lyric
sketches, O'Flaherty uses large substructures such as the
origins of capitalism, the development of a religious belief, or the refusal of men to barter spontaneity and freedom for security. He has written only a few stories that
might be called comprehensive fables or parables, but
these few make up some of his best work and are frequently anthologized.

Perhaps the best known of the comprehensive fables
is "Two Lovely Beasts," which demonstrates the effect
of greed on a peasant community and at the same time
might be interpreted as a fable on the origins of capitalism. In a rural setting, traditional regulations enforc-
ing cooperation dissolve because an individual flouts
custom, allows an insatiable greed to grow within himself, and, in a way, introduces the community to a
simple form of capitalism. The changes in the individual, the family, and the community have the implications that one associates with the best modern short
stories. Colm Derrane is a simple peasant with a strong
will, living in an impoverished part of the west of
Ireland. Here neighbor helps neighbor no matter how
little there is to share. Colm is importuned by Kate
Higgins, a penniless widow, to buy her two calves be-

cause the cow has died; no one in the village has the
money to buy the calves, nor has anyone enough milk
to feed them. Attracted by the sleekness of the animals,
Colm gives in to the widow's pleas. A chorus character,
Old Gorum, warns Colm that he is breaking the law by
depriving his neighbors and his family of milk in order
to feed the two calves. According to Old Gorum, whoever stands alone to work for his own profit becomes the
enemy of all the rest. Colm Derrane is then ostracized
even though he has helped the widow Higgins; he no
longer has a voice in the informal council of the land-
owners. Colm forces his family to eat limpets and peri-
winkles so that he may buy grass for the calves. Once
started on his enterprise, Colm cannot be restrained.
Up to the time of buying the calves, he had been governed by his wife, and she begins to complain about the
undernourished children. One day she attacks Colm
with tongs, a favorite weapon in marital disputes in
O'Flaherty. But Colm subdues her and beats her severely, and wife and children thereafter are subservient
to him.

Colm's prosperity now attracts the villagers and they
readmit him to their circle. Encouraged by his rise in
station among his neighbors, Colm next determines to
open a shop. Again he stints his family on food and
clothes. Because of the war, he finds a ready market for
the foodstuffs that he accumulates. But the shop succeeds so well that the villagers again become envious;
Colm has risen too far above them for neighborly con-
versation. The change in Colm is marked by a hardness,
a withering of the affections: "His gaunt face looked
completely unaware of their jeers. His pale blue eyes

stared fixedly straight ahead, cold and resolute and ruthless." Within a peasant setting, O'Flaherty shows the
effect of an initial act of greed and charity that leads to
a momentous change for individual and community.

Another comprehensive fable, "The Fairy Goose,"
may not compress all the history of religion as Frank
O'Connor once said, but it again utilizes the simple,
permanent world of peasants to dramatize a cycle of a
religious belief. O'Flaherty follows the rise and fall of a
myth in a community, similar to the rise and fall of
Christy Mahon's myth of killing his father in *The Play-
boy of the Western World*. In its brief compass, "The
Fairy Goose" shows the perverse ingenuity of man, his
gullibility, a cruelty in suppressing opposition under the
guise of righteousness, a degeneration once a myth has
been removed, and a nostalgia for a happiness never
possessed.

In "The Fairy Goose," Mary Wiggins owns a scraggly
gosling that is near death. Forestalled by a husband who
calls it a crime to kill anything that God has created for
his house, she watches the stunted gosling sympathetically. Gradually she comes to believe that the gosling
is spared because it is a fairy. She ties pink and red ribbons around its neck and sprinkles holy water on its
wing feathers. In the village, the gosling becomes un-
touchable; it is given food in every house. Soon people
bring dreams for interpretation. When children are ill,
the gosling is brought at night and led three times
around the house on a halter of horsehair.

Mrs. Wiggins starts to build a future around the gosling. She sets spells, trading them for cloth, sugar, and
potatoes. As an enchantress, she learns to roll her eyes

and mutter unintelligible sounds. Soon she is a woman
of wisdom. But Mrs. Wiggins has not anticipated the
fury of the local priest. Hearing of the miracles of the
gosling, the priest tries to turn it into an evil thing in
the eyes of the villagers. When the priest comes to her
house, Mrs. Wiggins goes into the yard and chants.
Calling her a hag, the priest strikes and fells her, taking
the ribbons from the goose. That night young men en-
tice the goose from its yard and stone it to death. From
that day the villagers become quarrelsome drunkards.
The only good time in the village, the people say, was
that in which the fairy goose was loved by the people.

In his stories, O'Flaherty's approach is that of the
storyteller consumed with his narrative; he has significant or amusing people and events to talk about; he
seems driven to move forward rapidly. He weaves in the
briefest description, characterization, or comment; he
eschews a piling up of detail. He reveres the present;
his characters do not look forward or backward, nor do
they indulge in reverie. This omnipotent present demands all of the narrator's energies, and so, despite his
Communistic leanings, O'Flaherty avoids propaganda,
a lesson apparently derived from his early training from
Edward Garnett. Even when the situation might tempt
him, as in "The Tramp," one of his best stories, he
stresses the opposition between educated men who
cling to the wretched routine of the workhouse instead
of accepting the invitation of a tramp to revel in the
freedom of the roads. In this story the grimness of the
workhouse stands out as a natural event, not as a result
of capitalism.

O'Flaherty's accomplishment in the short story lies

in the immediacy with which his lyric sketches and comprehensive fables present uncomplicated emotions and
instincts. In these stories O'Flaherty foregoes the intri-
cate craft of modern fiction as he searches for an elemental form to convey his experience. He searches,
often with admirable success, for an accurate expression
of these instincts and emotions. Only by attending pas-
sionately to raw experience can O'Flaherty produce a
literary effect. By relying on an ancient and simple
narrative form, O'Flaherty reveals again the adaptability
of man's love for direst narrative.

O'Flaherty records in his short stories vignettes of
peasants, children, and animals; he fashions images of a
life that seems timeless; men and nature function under
laws that cannot be altered by legislatures or technology.
In his novels, O'Flaherty examines peasant life not from
a timeless perspective but in its historical setting, showing the peasant in transition to a society in which money,
government, and Church play determining roles. In
Thy Neighbour's Wife, Skerrett, and other novels he
portrays people caught in changes that they cannot com-
prehend. Yet this historical study, valuable as it may
be, provides a background for enlarged characters who
wrestle with distorted dreams of perfection that are
often obsessions that betray and destroy them. In several
novels he portrays types of fanaticism that flourished in
the new Free State as disillusionment captures the mind
of men who had been unduly exhilarated from expec-
tations of national freedom.

Like Lawrence and other modern writers, O'Flaherty
tries to reconstruct images that recall man's instinctual
life. He pursues his task energetically, as he must if he

is to avoid the paralysis arising from passivity, violence, or sentimentality. As an artist, O'Flaherty is engaged, then, in the creation of cultural images, temporary though they may be, to supply what the civilization does not furnish—cultural images that lead to an integration of personality or, in Yeats's terms, to a unity of being. Beneath O'Flaherty's absorption in the physical, external world lies a belief in the evolutionary process, of men, especially artists, finding fulfillment in the struggle for perfection. This perfection may be elusive, even nonexistent, but nevertheless it is still the highest goal for man.

Selected Bibliography

NOVELS

Thy Neighbour's Wife. London: Jonathan Cape, 1923; New York: Boni & Liveright, 1924.

The Black Soul. London: Jonathan Cape, 1924; New York: Boni & Liveright, 1925.

The Informer. London: Jonathan Cape, 1925; New York: Alfred A. Knopf, 1925.

Mr. Gilhooley. London: Jonathan Cape, 1926; New York: Harcourt, Brace & Co., 1927.

The Assassin. London: Jonathan Cape, 1928; New York: Harcourt, Brace & Co., 1928.

The House of Gold. London: Jonathan Cape, 1929; New York: Harcourt, Brace & Co., 1929.

The Return of the Brute. London: Mandrake Press, 1929; New York: Harcourt, Brace & Co., 1930.

The Puritan. London: Jonathan Cape, 1931; New York: Harcourt, Brace & Co., 1932.

Skerrett. London: Gollancz, 1932; New York: R. Long & R. R. Smith, 1932.

The Martyr. London: Gollancz, 1932.

Hollywood Cemetery. London: Gollancz, 1935.

Famine. London: Gollancz, 1937; New York: Random House, 1937.

Land. London: Gollancz, 1946; New York: Random House, 1946.

Insurrection. London: Gollancz, 1950; Boston: Little, Brown & Co., 1951.

COLLECTIONS OF SHORT STORIES

Spring Sowing. London: Jonathan Cape, 1924; New York: Alfred A. Knopf, 1926.

The Tent. London: Jonathan Cape, 1926.

The Mountain Tavern and Other Stories. London: Jonathan Cape, 1929; New York: Harcourt, Brace & Co., 1929.

The Short Stories of Liam O'Flaherty. London: Jonathan Cape, 1937.

Two Lovely Beasts and Other Stories. New York: Devin-Adair, 1950.

The Stories of Liam O'Flaherty. New York: Devin-Adair, 1956.

Duil [In Gaelic]. Dublin: Sairseal Agus Dill, 1952.

AUTOBIOGRAPHY

Two Years. London: Jonathan Cape, 1930; New York: Harcourt, Brace & Co., 1930.

I Went to Russia. London: Jonathan Cape, 1931; New York: Harcourt, Brace & Co., 1931.

Shame the Devil. London: Grayson and Grayson, 1934.

BIOGRAPHY

The Life of Tim Healy. London: Jonathan Cape, 1927; New York: Harcourt, Brace & Co., 1927.

ARTICLES, REVIEWS, AND LETTERS TO EDITORS

"Art Criticism." *Irish Statesman* 9 (October 1, 1927) :83.

"Autobiographical Note." *Ten Contemporaries.* Edited by J. Gawsworth. 2nd series. London: 1933.

Foreword to *The Stars, The World, and The Women,* by Rhys Davies. London: William Jackson, 1930.

Introduction to *Six Cartoons,* by Alfred Lowe. London: W. & G. Foyle, 1930.

"The Irish Censorship." *American Spectator* 1 (November, 1932) : 2.

"Irish Housekeeping." *New Statesman and Nation* 11 (February 8, 1936) : 186.

"Kingdom of Kerry." *Fortnightly Review* 138 (August, 1932) : 212–18.

"Literary Criticism in Ireland." *Irish Statesman* 6 (September 4, 1926) : 711.

"Mr. Tasker's Gods." *Irish Statesman* 3 (March 7, 1925) : 460–61.

"My Life of Adventure." *TP's Weekly* 10 (October 20, 1928) : 756.

"My Experiences (1896–1923)." *Now and Then,* no. 10 (December, 1923), 14–15.

"The Plough and the Stars." *Irish Statesman* 5 (February 20, 1926) : 739–40.

"Red Ship." *New Republic* 68 (September 23, 1931) : 147–50.

"A View of Irish Culture." *Irish Statesman* 4 (1925) : 460–61.

"Writing in Gaelic." *Irish Statesman* 9 (December 17, 1927): 348.

POEMS

"Samaointe i geein" [Distant Thoughts]. *Dublin Magazine* 2 (December, 1924) : 330.

"The Blow." *Bell* 19 (May, 1954) : 9–22.

"Desire." *Bell* 19 (July, 1954) : 48–50.

"The Sniper." *Scholastic* 69 (October 18, 1956) : 18.

LIMITED EDITIONS

Civil War. London: E. Archer, 1925.

The Terrorist. London: E. Archer, 1926.

The Child of God. London: E. Archer, 1926.

Darkness (A Play). London: E. Archer, 1926; Also published in *New Coterie*, no. 3 (Summer, 1926) , pp. 42–68.

The Fairy-Goose and Two Other Stories. London: Crosby Gaige, 1927.

Red Barbara and Other Stories: The Mountain Tavern, Prey, The Oar. London: Crosby Gaige, 1928.

A Tourist's Guide to Ireland. London: Mandrake Press, 1930.

Joseph Conrad: An Appreciation. London: E. Lahr, 1930.

A Cure for Unemployment. London: E. Lahr, 1931.

The Ecstasy of Angus. London: Joiner & Steele, 1931.

The Wild Swan and Other Stories. London: Joiner & Steele, 1932.

Autobiographical Note. London: Gawsworth, 1933.

LETTERS

Liam O'Flaherty's Letters to Edward Garnett, May 5, 1923 to March 3, 1932. Manuscript Collection of the Academic Center Library, University of Texas, Austin, Texas.

CRITICAL STUDIES

Bates, H. E. *Edward Garnett*. London: Max Parrish, 1950.
————. *The Modern Short Story*. London: Thomas Nelson and Sons, 1945.

Beachcroft, T. O. *The Modest Art*. London: Oxford University Press, 1968.

Broderick, John. "Liam O'Flaherty: A Partial View." *Hibernia* 33 (December 19, 1969) : 17.

Canedo, Anthony. "Liam O'Flaherty: Introduction and Analysis." Dissertation, University of Washington (Seattle), 1965.

Colum, Padraic. "The Black Soul" [Review]. *The Saturday Review of Literature*, May 30, 1925, p. 787.

Davies, Rhys. Introduction to *The Wild Swan and Other Stories*, by Liam O'Flaherty. London: Joiner & Steele, 1932.

Doyle, Paul A. *Liam O'Flaherty*. New York: Twayne, 1972.

Emery, L. K. "A Primitive" [Review of *The Black Soul*]. *To-Morrow* 1 (August, 1924) : 7.

Greene, David H. "New Heights." *Commonweal* 64 (June 29, 1956) : 328.

Griffin, Gerald. "Liam O'Flaherty." *The Wild Geese: Pen Portraits of Famous Irish Exiles*. London: Jarrolds Publishers, 1938.

Hackett, Francis. "Liam O'Flaherty as Novelist." *On Judging Books*. New York: John Day Co., 1947.

Hampton, Angeline A. "Liam O'Flaherty: Additions to the Checklist." *Eire-Ireland* 6 (Winter, 1971) : 87–94.

Hatcher, Harlan. "Motion Picture Drama: Liam O'Flaherty." *Modern Dramas*. Shorter edition. New York: Harcourt, Brace and Co., 1944.

Hughes, Riley. "Two Irish Writers." *America* 83 (September 2, 1950) : 560–61.

Hynes, Frank J. "The 'Troubles' in Ireland." *Saturday Review of Literature* 29 (May 25, 1946) : 12.

Jacobs, Lewis. *Rise of the American Film*. New York: Harcourt, Brace and Co., 1939.

Kelleher, John V. "Irish Literature Today." *Atlantic Monthly* 175 (March, 1945) : 70–76.

Kelly, Angeline. "O'Flaherty on the Shelf." *Hibernia* 34 (November 20, 1970) : 8.

Kiely, Benedict. "Liam O'Flaherty: A Story of Discontent." *Month* New series 2 (September, 1949) : 183–93.

————. *Modern Irish Fiction—A Critique*. Dublin: Golden Eagle Books, 1950.

MacDonagh, Donagh. Afterword to *The Informer*, by Liam O'Flaherty. New York: New American Library, 1961.

Mercier, Vivian. Introduction to *The Stories of Liam O'Flaherty*, by Liam O'Flaherty. New York: Devin-Adair, 1956.

————. "The Irish Short Story and Oral Tradition." *The Celtic Cross*. Lafayette, Indiana: University of Purdue Press, 1964.

————. "Man Against Nature: The Novels of Liam O'Flaherty." *Wascana Review* 1 (1966) : 37–46.

Murray, Michael H. "Liam O'Flaherty and the Speaking Voice." *Studies in Short Fiction* 5 (Winter, 1968) : 154–62.

Neol [Leon O'Broin]. "An Dorchadas [The Darkness], an original play by Liam O'Flaherty." *Fainne an lae,* March 13, 1926, p. 6.

O'Casey, Sean. *Inishfallen, Fare Thee Well*. New York: Macmillan Co., 1960.

O'Connor, Frank. *The Lonely Voice*. New York: World Publishing Co., 1962.

O'Faolain, Sean. "Don Quixote O'Flaherty." *London Mercury* 37 (December, 1937) : 170–75; this article appears, with some modifications, in *Bell* 2 (June, 1941) : 28–36.

————. "Fifty Years of Irish Writing." *Studies* 51 (Spring, 1962) : 102–3.

Paul-Dubois, L. "Un romancier realiste en Erin: M. Liam

O'Flaherty." *Revue de Deux Monde* 21 (June 15, 1934) : 884, 904.

Pritchett, V. S. "Skerrett." *New Statesman and Nation* 4 1932) : 103.

Rosati, Salvatore. "Letterature Inglese." *Nuova Antologia* 69 (September 16, 1934) : 317–19.

Saul, George Brandon. "A Wild Sowing: The Short Stories of Liam O'Flaherty." *A Review of English Literature* 4 (July, 1963) : 108–13.

S.L.M. "The Informer" [Review]. *Irish Statesman* 5 (1925) : 148.

Theo. "Dorchadas—tuairim eile [*The Darkness*—another opinion]." *Fainne an lae,* March 13, 1926, p. 6.

Troy, William. "The Position of Liam O'Flaherty." *Bookman* [New York] 69 (March, 1929) : 7–11.

———. "Two Years." *Bookman* [New York] 72 (November, 1930) : 322–23.

Von Sternemann, J. "Irishe Geschicten: Novellen von Liam O'Flaherty." *Die Neue Rundschau* 42 (April, 1931) : 521–39.

Warren, C. Henry. "Liam O'Flaherty." *Bookman* [London] 77 (January, 1930) : 235–36.

Y. O. "The Assassin." *Irish Statesman* 10 (1928) : 295.

———. "The House of Gold." *Irish Statesman* 13 (1929) : 76.

———. "Mr. Gilhooley." *Irish Statesman* 7 (1926) : 279–80.

Zneimer, John N. "Liam O'Flaherty: The Pattern of Spiritual Crisis in his Art." Dissertation, University of Wisconsin, 1966.

———. *The Literary Vision of Liam O'Flaherty.* Syracuse: Syracuse University Press, 1970.

BIBLIOGRAPHY

Doyle, P. A. "A Liam O'Flaherty Checklist." *Twentieth Century Literature* 13 (April, 1967) : 49–51.

Doyle, P. A. *Liam O'Flaherty: An Annotated Bibliography.* Troy, N.Y.: Whitston, 1972.